Praise for
And the Lord Opened Her Eyes

The book *AND THE LORD OPENED HER EYES*, is a sophisticated piece in which the author relies on the story of Sarah's maid (Hagar), and her experience in the wilderness of Beersheba with her son, Ishmael, tries to show how blind many Christians have become, and how much they need to know their state of blindness and the remedy for it. Hagar wept, watching her son dying of dehydration. She did not relent. The reality of it is "Call upon me in the Day of trouble, and I will answer you and show you mighty and great things you do not know" (Jer. 33:3). God would always hear one who lifts his/her voice, especially while in the "wilderness of Beersheba" like Hagar. Christians can make it, whatever the situation may be, so long as they remain determined and rely on the word of God. He has used well-researched experiences of men and women of varying backgrounds to show that disability is not a hindrance. A consistent walk with God and His Son, Jesus Christ, according to the author is the sine-qua-non to extraordinary achievement and fulfillment in our present world.

The author has penned down the experience of men and women within and without Biblical records to encourage the reader to be open to God's revelation, without which we shall remain blind to numerous possibilities surrounding us, and which if we rightly or correctly approach will lead us to greater breakthroughs and successes in life.

Prof. Madu O. Iwe, CFS, FNIFST
National Chairman, S.U. Nigeria
Vice-Chancellor of Michael Okpara University,
Umudike, Umuahia, Abia State.

With the responsibility of the office that I hold, reading, which has been a lifelong hobby for me, has slowly taken backstage. When I came across this book *AND THE LORD OPENED HER EYES*, I honestly felt I would be leaving it on the first few pages, but as I started, I got glued as I scrolled page after page. If you seek productivity and enduring fulfillment through work, then this book should certainly be on your required reading list.

AND THE LORD OPENED HER EYES is a call in the face of limitations, to be wildly passionate, fearlessly reaching, and implausibly committed to your goals while slowly banishing all feeble excuses along the path of your creativity. In the light of the daunting challenges faced in today's society, I endorse this book for every employee, entrepreneur, and young business person who desires to excel and emphatically impact his generation. Great things are birthed out of our daily human frustrations and limitations. The message from God to us remains: "For a great and effective door has opened to me, and *there are* many adversaries" (1 Cor. 16:9). May God, through this book, open our eyes to the great opportunities that are available to us.

Engr Clement Onyeaso Nze,
Director-General/Chief Executive Officer,
Nigeria Hydrological Services Agency (NIHSA) &
Hydrological Adviser to the Permanent
Representative of Nigeria with World
Meteorological Organization (WMO)

God has a purpose for every human being, and there is a raging battle against destinies that stops only at one's death. Survival and success, which remain the abiding desires of for every individual, is not dependent on one's site (location), but on one's sight. Yes, what you can see can change our situation for good.

The book, *AND THE LORD OPENED HER EYES* is the need of this generation, that is full of young men and women whose destinies are under attack, but who unfortunately are hindered by blindness. I invite you to read this book; the LORD will use it to open your eyes and completely heal your blindness. Then shall you not die, but live to fulfil your destiny.

Nnamdigadi Chigor
Professor of Environmental and Public Health Microbiology,
Department of Microbiology, Faculty of Biological Sciences,
University of Nigeria, Nsukka 410001 Nigeria

This book ought to be adopted as an addendum, a backup or clarifier, to some other religious publications as they, invariably, tend to omit the whole essence of the Bible. To interpret and apply the Bible correctly, one requires divine understanding. The author has conscientiously shown the delimiting effects of spiritual blindness and lack of inspiration and demonstrated with apt examples how we can overcome the challenges of life. The book is highly recommended, in view of the eroding moral standards of our time; not as an alternative to the Bible, itself, due to intellectualistic exegesis, but for its clearer and more practical interpretation, based on moral 'thisness.'

Lawrence C. Igboekwe.

"Your eye is the lamp of your body. When your eye is healthy, your whole body is full of light, but when it is bad, your body is full of darkness" (Luke 11:34).

And The LORD Opened Her Eyes is loaded with scripture and takes the reader through a cross section of testimonies that show the benefits of living fully by depending on God.

To make it even easier to grasp, the author has dissected every day occurrences and terms to bring forth quickly through the eye-gate precious vital truth based on the Word of God.

This book was done solely for the purpose of glorifying our Lord Jesus Christ. Emphasis is given on the subject of sight for the purpose of quickly enlightening God's people who seem to be "falling away" from true faith in our Lord Jesus Christ and to prevent the unfruitful drift towards the distractions of modernism in our world today. It challenges the reader to operate at the highest level commensurate with our calling in Christ Jesus.

Faye Nwoko
USA

For one thing, this book is inspirational; first, for creative or inquisitive minds. Second, it engenders thinking about "me." Am I endowed with a creative mind, ability, and gifts? What are those innate creative abilities I have? How do I discover these potentials, as to tap into them to help solve humanities challenges? The book points the answer comes from God, the author of creative instincts.

Dr. Nwachukwu G. William
Cybersecurity Official.
Alabama, USA.

AND THE LORD OPENED HER EYES

by
J.C. AGUNWAMBA

Published by KHARIS PUBLISHING, imprint of KHARIS MEDIA LLC.

Copyright © 2022 J.C. Agunwamba

ISBN-13: 978-1-63746-143-3

ISBN-10: 1-63746-143-7

Library of Congress Control Number: 2022940474

All rights reserved. This book or parts thereof may not be reproduced in any form, stored in a retrieval system, or transmitted in any form by any means - electronic, mechanical, photocopy, recording, or otherwise - without prior written permission of the publisher, except as provided by United States of America copyright law.

Scripture taken from THE HOLY BIBLE, NEW INTERNATIONAL VERSION ®. Copyright© 1973, 1978, 1984, 2011 by Biblica, Inc.™. Used by permission of Zondervan

All KHARIS PUBLISHING products are available at special quantity discounts for bulk purchase for sales promotions, premiums, fund-raising, and educational needs. For details, contact:

Kharis Media LLC

Tel: 1-479-599-8657

support@kharispublishing.com

www.kharispublishing.com

Table of Contents

FOREWORD xiii
BEAUTY OF BLINDNESS 17
    1.1 Introduction 17
    1.2 Appreciation of God's Blessings 20
    1.3 Appreciation of the Gift of Good EyeSight 20
PHYSICAL BLINDNESS 22
    2.1 Complete Blindness 22
    2.2 Color Blindness 23
    2.3 Night Blindness 24
    2.4 Trachoma 24
    2.5 River blindness 24
    2.6 Cataracts 24
    2.7 Reflective Errors 25
    2.8 Glaucoma 25
SPIRITUAL BLINDNESS 26
    3.1 Introduction 26
    3.2 Complete Blindness 27
    3.3 Partial Blindness 28
        3.3.1 New Born Again Christian 28
        3.3.2 Distorted Sight 28
        3.3.3 Night Blinded Christians 29
        3.3.4 Color Blind Christian 30
GOD'S WAYS OF BLESSING HIS CHILDREN 32
    4.1 Introduction 32
    4.2 Existence of a Problem 33
    4.3 Transfer of Wealth 35
    4.4 Gifts and Talents 36

4.5 Use of Other Creatures 37
INNOVATION 39
   5.1. Introduction 39
   5.2 Definition 40
   5.3 Source of Our Creativity 42
   5.4 Purpose of creativity 43
   5.5 Benefits of Creativity 45
   5.6 Examples of Creativity in the Scriptures 47
   5.7 God's Way of Giving Inspiration 48
      5.7.1 Prayers 48
      5.7.2 Believe 55
      5.7.3 Act on the idea and do not be lazy. 55
      5.7.4 Create time to relax and think. 57
   5.8 Approaches for Unlocking our Potentials 57
      5.8.1. Recognize that creativity comes from God 57
      5.8.2. Understand your creative role 58
      5.8.3. Feed your inner artisan 58
      5.8.4. Write it all down 58
      5.8.5. Know your internal clock 58
   5.9. Ways of Getting Inspired Ideas 59
      5.9.1 Direct Revelation from God 59
      5.9.2 Dreams 60
      5.9.3 Analysis of Human System 64
      5.9.4 Other God's Creature 64
GENERATION OF IDEAS USING HUMAN TECHNIQUES 72
   6.1 Introduction 72
      6.1.1 Rules of Brainstorming (Alex Osborn's Applied Imagination) 73
   6.2 Eight Ways To Generate More Ideas In A Group 74
   6.3 Other Techniques 75
      6.3.1 SCAMPER 75
      6.3.2. Brainstorming 76

6.3.3. Mind mapping 76
6.3.4. Synectics 77
6.3.5. Storyboarding 77
6.3.6. Roleplaying 77
6.3.7. Attribute listing 78
6.3.8. Visualization and visual prompts 78
6.3.9. Morphological analysis 78
6.3.10. Forced relationships 79
6.3.11 Daydreaming 79
6.3.12. Reverse thinking 79
6.3.13. Questioning assumptions 79
6.3.14 Accidental genius 80
6.3.15. Brainwriting 80
6.3.16 Wishing 80
6.3.17 Socializing 80
6.3.18 Collaboration 81
6.3.19 Using analogies 81
6.4. Thomas Edison's Example 82
6.5 Areas We Need God to Open Our Eyes 85
6.5.1 Security 85
6.5.2 Amory 85
6.5.3 Military Intelligence 86
6.6 Technology 87
6.7 Business 87
ENHANCING OUR ABILITY TO RECEIVE REVELATION 88
7.1 Introduction 88
7.2 Beam Versus Specks 88
7.3 Singleness of Purpose 89
7.4 Viewing Position 89
7.5 Clarity of Vision 91
POSITIVE ATTITUDES TOWARD SUCCESS 92

8.1 Lift up Your Eyes 92
8.2 Looking for A city 93
8.3 The Nature of Revelation..94
    8.3.1 God's Ways Are Unpredictable.....................................94
    8.3.2 Little Fishes 94
    8.3.3 God Wants to Open Your Eyes 94
8.4 Deceitfulness 97
    8.4.1 Deception of Riches 98
MEDITATION 99
9.1 Introduction 99
9.2 Brings us closer to God...102
9.3 Transforms 103
9.4 Removes Anxiety and Solves Health Problems............103
    9.4.1 Helps us Gain Control Over Our thoughts 104
9.5 Key to Success 104
9.6 It Builds Faith...105
9.7 Gives Access to Inspired Ideas 105
9.8 Power of the Human Mind..107
    9.8.1 Unlimited Capacity...107
    9.8.2 Information Processing..107
    9.8.3 Creativity..108
    9.8.4 Dictates Our lives..108
9.9 Power of the Brain 109
9.10 The Treasure base 109
9.11 Improving the Mind..110
CALL UPON HIM 113
10.1 Introduction 113
10.2 His Son Jesus..113
10.3 Innovation through Revelation 115
10.4 Enlarging Our Minds for Innovation - Come Apart and Rest 117
    10.4.1 Social Life 117

10.4.2 Improves Leadership Skills 118
10.2.4 Boosts Self Confidence 119
10.2.5 Increases Focus and Attention 119
10.2.6 Reduction in Anger 119
LORD, OPEN MY EYES 121
  11.1 Introduction 121
  11.2. See God's Promise 123
  11.3 Revelation of the Riches of Christ 125
  11.4 Revelation of His glory 126
  11.5 Revelation of Jesus 126
  11.6 Revelation of Our position in Christ 127
    11.6.1 Translation 127
    11.6.2 Magnification 128
    11.6.3 Rotation 128
    11.6.4 Inversion 129
    11.5.5 Essence of transformation 129
GREAT STEPS FOR RECEIVING REVELATIONS 131
  12.1 Great Revelations 131
  12.1 She remained 132
  12.2 She stooped low 133
  12.3 She looked 133
  12.4 She saw 134
  12.5 She heard 134
  CONCLUSION 135
  REFERENCES 136
    About Kharis Publishing: 139

FOREWORD

Sarah saw Ishmael, the son of Hagar scoffing at Isaac. She demanded from her husband, Abraham, "Cast out this bondwoman and her son; for the son of this bondwoman shall not be heir with my son, namely Isaac" (Gen. 21:9-10).

God of heaven backed Sarah's demand and spoke to Abraham, "Do not let it be displeasing in your sight because of the lad or because of your bondwoman. Whatever Sarah has said to you, listen to her voice; for in Isaac your seed shall be called."

That was strange! But the will of God stands. Hagar had to go through a tough experience with her son, Ishmael, who must be separated from the son of promise for the eyes of Hagar to be opened. So, Abraham rose early in the morning and took bread and a skin of water. Putting it on her shoulder, he sent them away. Then she departed (blindly) and wandered in the wilderness of Beersheba (Gen. 21:14).

After some time, the water in the skin was used up and their suffering started. In her distress, she desired death for the boy. She lifted her voice and wept and God heard the voice of the boy and responded to their distress. "What ails you, Hagar? Fear not, for God has heard the voice of the lad where he is. Arise, lift up the lad and hold him with your hand, for I will make him a great nation." "And God opened her eyes, she saw a well of water" (Gen. 21:19).

The book **AND THE LORD OPENED HER EYES**, is a sophisticated piece in which the author relies on the story of Sarah's maid (Hagar), and her experience in the wilderness of Beersheba with her son, Ishmael, tries to show how blind many Christians have become, and how much they need to know their state of blindness and the remedy for it. The reality is that physical challenges are no longer issues in the world today. Blindness, lameness, etc., have not prevented determined men and women from achieving their set goals and greatness. Hagar wept, watching her son dying of dehydration. She did not relent. Today we can refer to her disposition as Pray Until Something Happens (PUSH). The reality of it is "Call upon me in the Day of trouble, and I will answer you and show you mighty and great things you do not know" (Jer. 33:3). The beauty of Moses' ministry was the power of his intercession for the recalcitrant people of Israel. A ministry that is fast fading in the Church today among the priests and ministers, because their attention has been diverted from the people who should be their focus to trivialities of fame, money, and power. God would always hear one who lifts his/her voice, especially while in the "wilderness of Beersheba" like Hagar. Gen. 21:19 happens to be the center point of this book: "And God opened her eyes, and she saw a well of water;" not a skin of water.

Prof. Jonah Agunwamba has raised a lot of encouraging thoughts in **"And the Lord opened her eyes"** to show that Christians can make it, whatever the situation may be, so long as they remain determined and rely on the word of God. He has used well-researched experiences of men and women of varying backgrounds to show that disability is not a hindrance. A consistent walk with God and His Son, Jesus Christ, according to the author is the sine-qua-non to extraordinary achievement and fulfillment in our present world.

He opines with Ortiz that "the mighty deeds of God are everywhere, but the trouble is that we do not see them (blindness). The experience of the disciples on the road to Emmaus stands out in many of our personal/daily experiences. They walked with Jesus a distance of several kilometers hearing His voice without recognizing him. This has been a lot for many Christians, especially those who cannot raise their voice and cry out like Hagar - **"Let me not see the death of the boy."** The Scripture surely stated that what we desire and speak to God about, that shall He do (Mark 11:24). In the same way, what we dream about, plan for, and purposefully pursue, that we shall attain in our life's time. The author has penned down the experience of men and women within and without Biblical records to encourage the reader to be open to God's revelation, without which we shall remain blind to numerous possibilities surrounding us, and which if we rightly or correctly approach will lead us to greater breakthroughs and successes in life.

Prof. Madu O. Iwe, CFS, FNIFST
National Chairman, S.U. Nigeria
Vice-Chancellor of Michael Okpara University,
Umudike, Umuahia, Abia State.

CHAPTER ONE

BEAUTY OF BLINDNESS

1.1 Introduction

In the past, most people who were incapacitated by one sickness or the other still contributed immensely to societal growth despite their physical challenges. The same is true today. Blindness, lameness, and other physical challenges have not prevented determined men and women from achieving greatness. A challenging example was the composer, Fanny Crosby. Her total blindness, which began just a few months after birth, added to the richness and depth of the words she wrote.[1] Several other blind people, such as George Matheson, William Walford, and others, wrote some of the most remarkable hymns of our Christian heritage. The annals of history are full of names of people who, despite their disabilities, became famous hymn writers. Early in life, Charlotte Elliot's severe illness condemned her to a frustrated bedridden life of wriggling in pains. As a young girl, she would lament that her physical problems left her irritable and out of sorts. But after she opened her life to Christ, she wrote the wonderful hymn, "Just as I Am." Catherine Hankey,

---

[1] Bradbury, W. (1913). Fanny Crosby in Heroines of Modern Religion. Ed. Foster, W.D. Sturgis & Walton Co., New York.
Fanny Crosby. Prolific and Blind hymn writer. Christian History.
https://www.christianitytoday.com/history/people/poets/fanny-crosby.html
(2010) Fanny Crosby: America's Hymn Queen.
https://www.christianity.com/church/church-history/timeline/1801-1900/fanny-crosby-americas.hymn.

confined to bed to recover from a severe illness, wrote "Tell Me the Old, Old story" Eliza Hewitt had a painful spinal condition. The song "When We All get to Heaven "came from her excruciating pain." Disability, illness, frail health, and other forms of health challenges marked the great hymn writers of the faith. Even William Cowper had a severe mental illness, and he wrote, "There Is a Fountain Filled with Blood." And who can forget the story of Horatio Spafford, who composed "It is Well with My Soul" after he lost four daughters in a terrible shipwreck?

The mighty things the physically challenged do, how they could free themselves from the crippling emotional pains inflicted by their circumstances and soar on high like the eagle and achieve something for God to the amazement of all, are sources of great encouragement to me. Their conditions and the way they bear it have taught me one thing – it is well with my soul, no matter the life challenges facing me. While they have challenges, they have learned to draw strength from their inner man, energized and comforted by the Holy Spirit, who transports them beyond the physical and enables them to tap from the infinite reservoir of God's love. Their experience shows we can always live rich by depending on God, who is not limited whether by the extent of use or purpose by human thoughts, imaginations, and expectations. God often reveals great things to some of them, which, if we seek, without distractions from our 'abilities,' will also be ours. What they have, which many of us may lack, is the ability to have our inner eyes opened to receive revelations. Crosby believed her visual impairment added to the richness and depth of the words she wrote.

Born in Putnam County, New York, Crosby became ill within two months. Unfortunately, the family doctor was away, and another man—pretending to be a certified doctor—treated her by prescribing hot mustard poultices to be applied to her eyes. Her illness eventually relented, but the treatment left her blind. By the time the doctor was revealed to be a quack, he had disappeared. A few months later, Crosby's father died. Her mother was forced to work as a maid to support the family, and her Christian grandmother mostly raised Fanny.

Fanny had every right to be angry with her parents who invited the doctor without recognizing he was a quack; God for arranging her birth under such circumstances; the quack doctor for administering the wrong therapy. But she never did. Her love of poetry began early—her first verse, written at age 8, echoed her lifelong refusal to feel sorry for herself:

> Oh, what a happy soul I am,
> Although I cannot see!
> I am resolved that in this world
> Contented I will be.
> How many blessings do I enjoy
> That other people don't,
> To weep and sigh because I'm blind
> I cannot, and I won't!

She decided not to be weighed down by her circumstances and instead focused on the positive things. She praised God for granting her the opportunity to be blind. She gave thanks in everything, which is actually the will of God concerning us, which perks us up and opens us up to receive blessings. "If perfect earthly sight were offered me tomorrow," she said, "I would not accept it. I might not have sung hymns to the praise of God if I had been distracted by the beautiful and interesting things about me." According to biographer Annie Willis, "had it not been for her affliction, she might not have so good an education or have so great an influence, and certainly not so fine a memory.[2]" While she enjoyed her poetry, she zealously memorized the Bible. Memorizing five chapters a week, even as a child, she could recite the Pentateuch, the Gospels, Proverbs, the Song of Solomon, and many psalms chapter and verse.

When multitasking, the mind's power is diverted to multiple tasks. Hence, the output is not 100%. So, what you can do is concentrate on one thing. Even your senses take away a part of your brain, and you only have a small percentage of it to think and do stuff. For example, if you close your eyes and listen carefully, you can listen with better concentration and hear more clearly than when you open your eyes. It is because your mind was processing the information it was receiving from the optic nerve, and when you close your eyes, your brain stops receiving the info from your eyes, focusing on other senses. Her blindness and disability helped her memorize and, I believe, meditate on the Word and empowered her brain to receive inspiration from God. Her ability to compose several songs was not unconnected with her renewing her mind and filling it with the Word of God. She was not the only one who was blind. But she decided to turn her disability into ability.

---

[2] Willis, A.I. (2001). A blind Hymn Writer. Daily True American, P.2

1.2 Appreciation of God's Blessings

Just as David said, God daily loads us with His blessings. "Bless (affectionately, gratefully praise) the Lord, O my soul; and forget not one of all His benefits – Who forgives (every one of) all your iniquities ...Who beautifies, dignifies, and crowns you with loving-kindness and tender mercy; Who satisfies your mouth ...with good ..." (Psalm 103: 2 – 5 TAB). God is constantly caring for us in all areas of our lives, but we tend to forget all His benefits. Sometimes we remember a few, the so-called big ones in our estimation, and ignore others, which may, in reality, be more valuable. For instance, we often may not thank God for the gift of nature, the completeness of parts of our body, and the renewal of our strength while others of our age are bedridden. Likewise, we may forget to appreciate the gift of a good appetite to enjoy food until we become sick. I wonder how many of us consistently thank God for all the love He showers daily on us and doesn't forget some.

We eat, drink and put on clothes only to complain that we haven't some other things. We intend to worry about the minor issues in our lives, whereas we are supposed to be full of thanks to God. "Having food and raiment let us be contented; for we brought nothing to this world and we shall certainly leave with nothing" (1 Tim 6:8 KJV).

1.3 Appreciation of the Gift of Good EyeSight

Sometimes instead of appreciating God for His gifts, we misuse them. Instead of using our gift of Sight for good purposes, we use it for devilish ends. What we see stirs up strife, unconstructive criticisms, jealousy, and other evils. What God intended to be a blessing, happiness, and rich source of creativity and innovative ideas becomes a source of distraction and home for the occupation of evil thoughts.

Could we have been using God's blessing of physical wholesomeness and good Sight in particular for evil? The Scripture admonishes, "I beseech you, therefore, brethren that you present yourself as a living sacrifice holy and acceptable to God which is your reasonable sacrifice" (Rom. 12: 1, 2). Another verse says that we should yield our members as instruments of righteousness. It includes deploying our thoughts and minds to creative and productive activities instead of squandering them on evil things. "Whatever things are true; whatever things are honest; whatever things are just; whatever things are pure; whatever things are lovely; whatever things are of good report; if there is any virtue; if there is any praise, think on these things" (Phil. 4:8).

We may decide to see our adversity as a blessing and enjoy the favorable fruits of tapping strength from the Almighty God. He knows how to use it for our good. But, on the other hand, we may wallow in complaint and self-pity, blaming God and others for our predicament, and miss out on enjoying the glorious life of fulfilling our destiny and being a source of blessing to others.

Fanny's father caught a chill while working in the cold November rain and died soon after. Twenty-one-year-old Mercy Crosby was left to provide for herself and her daughter. She did this by seeking employment as a maid. Fanny's grandmother cared for her during the day, and the two became very close. Fanny would later write, "My grandmother was more to me than I can ever express by word or pen."

She maintained this positive outlook all her life and considered her blindness a blessing, not the curse many would be tempted to call it. "I think it is a great pity that the Master did not give you sight when he showered so many other gifts upon you," remarked one well-meaning preacher. Fanny Crosby responded at once. "Do you know that if at birth I had been able to make one petition, it would have been that I was born blind?" She asked and then said, "Because when I get to heaven, the first face that shall ever gladden my sight will be that of my Savior."

However, the author does not intend to show that the physically challenged are more able to achieve great success than those who are not. We should always treat disabilities medically if possible - or better, by exercising faith in God and the finished work of our Lord and Savior, Jesus Christ, who gave himself as a ransom for our peace, healings, and comfort.

CHAPTER TWO

PHYSICAL BLINDNESS

2.1 Complete Blindness

Complete blindness is the inability to see anything, even light. A partially blind person has limited vision. For example, he may have blurry vision or be unable to distinguish the shapes of objects. Complete blindness means that he cannot see at all.

Merck Manuals reports that legal blindness is equal to or worse than a 20/200 visual acuity in the better eye.[3] Having a visual acuity of 20/200 means that someone with normal vision can see an object at 200 feet, and a person with impaired vision can see at a distance no further than 20 feet.[4] Several different diseases can cause complete blindness; some develop later in life, and some are present at birth. The leading cause of blindness is diabetes. It causes diabetic retinopathy, which destroys the retina. Other causes of complete blindness include cataracts, which obstruct the light from hitting the retina because of opaque patches on a lens, and glaucoma, which causes blindness due to damage to the optic nerve. Age-related macular degeneration is the most common cause of blindness in adults who are 60 or older.

---

[3] Merck Manuals: Symptoms
[4] (2007) American optometric Association, color Deficiency. (17th July)
    Kozarsky, A. (2020). What does it mean to be legally blind? https://www.webmd.com/eye-health/legally-blind-meaning.2020.webMD, LLC.

2.2 Color Blindness

The different colors in each part of the rainbow correspond to a different wavelength of light. Reddish colors have a long wavelength. Bluish colors have a shorter one. Just as there are many notes on the piano, many wavelengths of light match the different colors.[5]

Color-blind people cannot distinguish specific colors, especially shades of red and green which are the most common type of color blindness. Color blindness is almost always present at birth and is usually caused by a defective gene on the X chromosome. More men are affected by color blindness than women because women have two X chromosomes; thus, even if they are "carriers" of a bad gene, their other X chromosome usually has a functional gene. Because men have only one X chromosome, the presence of one bad gene is sufficient to cause color blindness. Defective retinal cells result in some forms of color blindness; defects in the optic nerve cause other forms.

When the cones have all the various pigments - called photopigments – one sees all possible colors. If there's a problem with the pigments, one won't see colors the way one should. This condition is called color deficiency or color blindness.

Color blindness can lead to various safety concerns in almost any laboratory. Therefore, asking about it should be standard practice. Many laboratories already provide special safety glasses for people who need ordinary eyeglasses. Providing these glasses should be a natural extension of that type of policy.

Color blindness hinders the victims from reading the correct indicators in the traffic and caution lights and acting correctly. In addition, color blindness can result in several cases of humiliation and frustration like misinterpreting the color of a spouse's or friend's clothes, misjudging some furniture, etc.[6]

---

[5] Kozarsky, A. (2020). What does it mean to be legally blind? https://www.webmd.com/eye-health/legally-blind-meaning.2020.webMD, LLC.
   Jain, V. (2020). Are there types of Blindness? https://www.dragarwal.com/blog/contact-lens-and-low-vision/are-there-types-of-blindness/
[6] Jain, V. (2020). Are there types of Blindness? https://www.dragarwal.com/blog/contact-lens-and-low-vision/are-there-types-of-blindness/

2.3 Night Blindness

Night blindness is a vision impairment that occurs at night or when light is dim. It significantly impairs and makes the victim have difficulty driving at night or seeing stars. Rods only have one kind of pigment. It reacts the same way to any light wavelength. So, rods do not have anything to do with color vision. But they are susceptible to light and allow us to see at night.[7]

2.4 Trachoma

The world's leading infectious cause of blindness is trachoma. It starts as an eye infection, a bit like conjunctivitis. Over time it causes scarring to the eyelid that makes the eyelashes turn inward and scrape against the eye if it is not treated. This condition causes tremendous pain and, eventually, blindness. The infection can be treated with antibiotics, while surgery can stop the eyelashes from rubbing against the eyeball.[8]

2.5 River blindness

River blindness is a parasitic infection that can cause severe skin irritation, itching, visual impairment, and irreversible blindness. Also known as onchocerciasis, river blindness is spread by the bite of infected black flies that breed in fast-flowing rivers. Administering appropriate medication can help stop the spread of infection.[9]

2.6 Cataracts

A build-up of protein that clouds the eye's lens causes cataracts, leading to blurred vision and, eventually, blindness. Cataracts likely cause up to 60 percent of blindness in parts of Africa, and 20 million people worldwide are blind because of the condition.[10]

---

[7] Jain, V. (2020). Are there types of Blindness? https://www.dragarwal.com/blog/contact-lens-and-low-vision/are-there-types-of-blindness/
[8] https://www.who.int/news-room/fact-sheets/detail/trachoma
[9] http://www.who.int/news-room/fact-sheets/detail/onchocerciasis
[10] Centers for Disease Control and Prevention CDC 24/7: Saving Lives, Protecting People. https://www.cdc.gov/visionhealth/basics/ced/index.html

2.7 Reflective Errors

Reflective errors are caused by irregularity in the shape of the eye, making it hard to focus clearly. They include myopia, also called short-sightedness, and hyperopia, known as long-sightedness. Other types of eye diseases are stigmatism and presbyopia. An irregularly curved cornea causes sigmatism while presbyopia is a normal aging change where the eye can no longer focus at close range. These eye conditions can be particularly problematic in poorer developing countries, where those affected may not be able to afford sight tests or spectacles.[11]

2.8 Glaucoma

Blockage of the eye's drainage results in pressure that can damage the optic nerve and cause glaucoma.[12]

All the above blindness causes one defect or the other and limits the functions of the eye. And as was mentioned before, they impose some sort of limitations on the sufferer and prevent him from enjoying life to its fullest, especially when the sufferer refuses to adapt. Blindness is a disease that hinders a person from seeing. It restricts his association with people, vocational choice, the pleasure one could derive from seeing, and so on. Blindness disqualified priests from sacrificing or approaching the altar (Lev. 21:17–23) and rendered sacrificial animals unacceptable (Lev. 22:21–22; Deut. 15:21; Mal. 1:8).

---

[11] Centers for Disease Control and Prevention CDC 24/7: Saving Lives, Protecting People. https://www.cdc.gov/visionhealth/basics/ced/index.html
[12] Centers for Disease Control and Prevention CDC 24/7: Saving Lives, Protecting People. https://www.cdc.gov/visionhealth/basics/ced/index.html

CHAPTER THREE

SPIRITUAL BLINDNESS

3.1 Introduction

While physical blindness can help the sufferer focus inwards and tap from the treasures in his subconscious, spiritual blindness has no single advantage. Whereas there are several exhortations in the scriptures encouraging people to show mercy on the physically challenged, the Lord approached the spiritually blinded with rebuke and anger. It seems the spiritually blind are responsible for their state, whereas the physically blind might not be responsible for their predicament. Therefore, there is always an admonition for the spiritually blind to subject themselves to spiritual therapy and become enlightened.

Spiritual blindness will limit our relationship with God and our understanding of spiritual things. Sometimes physical blindness will restrict the extent one accomplishes his dreams, especially in some professions that involve active utilization of Sight and seeing others physically. But that is the much it can limit one. Spiritual blindness, on the other hand, can cause a Christian to miss God's will for his life entirely and limit the full development of his potential for the whole life span. Spiritual blindness may hinder us from knowing God's will for our lives; limit our perception, recognition, and appropriation of the great privileges and rights the death of Christ brought to us. Sometimes ugly events happened around us, taking us unawares, whereas if we had a revelation of them, we would have taken some measures to avert it. It can make us live stunted Christian life whereby we remain babies in the eyes of the Lord. Whereas we ought to be teachers, we need to be thought. In contrast, we should have been mature and be occupied with spiritual reproduction; we still grope about uncertain of our beliefs.

Revelation helps increase our confidence and trust in God. Receiving more revelations from God helps to boost our faith. Christianity is a practical way of living. As we contact the Spirit behind the Word, that aspect becomes real, and we do not need any person to teach us, because the Holy Spirit has already taught us. Aaron could not resist the Israelites' request to mold another god for themselves, because he had not had an experiential knowledge of God himself. All along, God spoke to him through Moses and not directly. If someone had asked Moses, "Moses, can God speak to man?" What do you think Moses would have answered? Now Imagine Aaron being asked the same question? He would have probably replied, "I don't know." In Christianity, experience helps to strengthen faith and belief. Without experience, Christianity reduces to the mere theoretical way of life without fruitfulness. Everybody is blind, either forever or only temporarily. The gospel offers light to the blind, the light of truth, the light of holiness and virtue through Christ. He alone is the light. Whoever follows Him will not walk in darkness.

Just as there are different kinds of physical blindness, there are also different levels of spiritual blindness. We present these below:

3.2 Complete Blindness

Complete blindness is a state where someone cannot see any spiritual truth from the scriptures or receive any revelation. The Bible is meaningless. It is a closed book. He can pick the scriptures and peruse them, but he does not get anything. The wordings are of no spiritual significance as far as he is concerned. He sees and interprets it like any other book. Because he never contacts life from it, it lacks sweetness. It is tedious, and he cannot enjoy it, like David said, "the word is like honey to me." This group can only interpret the scriptures at the moral level, just like any other person. The spiritual significance and lessons are unknown to him. So, every human being comes into the world blind in the darkness, being human. Add to the fact that sin compounds blindness (John 3:19 and 20 NKJV). "...men loved darkness rather than light because their deeds were evil." Everyone born into the world, being human, is cut off from spiritual reality. 1 Corinthians 2:14 says, "But the natural man does not receive the things of the Spirit of God, for they are foolishness to him, nor can he know them, because they are spiritually discerned," and he is spiritually dead.

According to 2 Corinthians 4:4, Satan aggravates the problem of spiritual blindness. The god of this world has blinded the unbelievers" minds such that the light of the glorious gospel will not shine on them. Sin and Satan blind man naturally. Profound blindness engulfs the souls of all human beings. It can also become sovereign blindness. There are illustrations of that in the ministry of our Lord Jesus and other places in the Scripture.

The leaders of Israel loved the darkness and hated the light. The people who followed them were in the same category. The leaders of Israel and the people who followed them were devoted to their delusion of self-righteousness, their delusion of ritualistic ceremonial legalistic religion.

3.3 Partial Blindness

3.3.1 New Born Again Christian

Once someone has become born again, God shines His light upon his soul, and whenever he reads the Bible with an open mind, he will understand it. The Scripture will no longer be closed to him. The Ethiopian Eunuch was studying the book of Isaiah when the Holy Spirit sent Philip, the Evangelist, to him; he did not understand the scriptures until Philip expounded them to him. One of the functions of the Holy Spirit is to explain the scriptures and teach the believer all truth. The unbeliever has not the Holy Spirit. He is like an orphan, groping about spiritually without the Holy Ghost to guide him. But once he becomes born again, the indwelling Holy Spirit quickens his Spirit, and he can then understand spiritual truths. However, though he is born again and now can see the truth, he will not see the truth all at once. God expects him to see more truths as days go by and as he develops his relationship with Him.

3.3.2 Distorted Sight

Several factors will affect how much revelation he receives, including his devotion to the Scriptures and obedience, all requiring his corporation. This is where the story of the gradual healing of the blind man becomes very relevant. Different Christians have different levels of blindness. They have different degrees of light passing through their eyes, allowing them limited views and understanding. That calls for greater exposure to the light of the scriptures and teachings and a desire to know more until we finally meet Him, and we shall be like Him. Paul said, "Oh! That I may know him..." In order words, Lord, I am blind. I cannot see you and your promises clearly. Men are like trees. And because I see them as trees, I relate to them that way. I do not love them as I should. I am very insensitive and unreasonable. I treat them like trees as if they do not have feelings. Lord, I need a second touch. Whenever a Christian does not have sympathetic feelings towards others and claims he is born again, if a man treats his wife, employees, or fellow workers like a piece of wood, it is only because he requires more touch from God. He could only treat people the way he sees them.

Another way the devil can penetrate through the life of a Christian is by making him see things only in parts. At each level of our development, there are things we ought to see that the Scripture tells us that will never be complete until we see Him and be like Him. However, at every stage of our growth, the devil can blind someone and only allow him as much light as could enable him to see things partly. He could see a man's head without seeing the legs or vice versa. Imagine how dangerous and traumatic such a 'hallucinating experience' can be. If he sees men as trees, he could chop them into firewood with a knife! Concerning the issues of life, such a condition will undoubtedly lead a child of God to live in an imaginary world of wrong expectations from people or having warped judgment or false assumptions where he thinks every other person is wrong except him. Only as the Lord opens our eyes can we escape this kind of bondage. The devil has blinded those that perish so that they will not see the truth and repent. We need to ask God to deliver us from all forms of partial blindness.

3.3.3 Night Blinded Christians

This category of Christians, though seeing, is blinded during the night of pressures of life. Lack and anxiety prevent them from getting revelations from the Word of God. Matthew 16:12 says that the minds of the disciples wandered away. Lack of bread is not an issue if we carefully follow His instructions. Church leaders should consider the welfare of the members under their care seriously. Lack of food or too much of it or poor distribution can reduce the extent of blessings church members receive from God. Those of us who preach the Word should also ensure equitable distribution of the physical goods that come to the church. Even though several instructions encourage us to trust and depend entirely on God for our sustenance, we continually forget the ability of God to take care of us. Sometimes, like the disciples, we are blind to the words we read in the scriptures. We are blind to the correct interpretations. Jesus says one thing, and we interpret or misconstrue it. We can't apply it correctly in one area of life without following the right prescription. Our preoccupation is with what to eat, drink, and put on. We often lack concentration when the sermon is going on.

Jesus asked them a series of rhetorical questions. "Do you not yet see or understand? Do you have a hardened heart? Having eyes, do you not see? Having ears, do you not hear?" They were familiar with all those statements because Jesus had already told them earlier that those things do not apply to the people from whom He has hidden the truth.[13] But He said as I quoted in Matthew 13, "To you it has been given to know the mysteries, to understand." And now He's saying, "Are you no better than they are? Are you as dark as they are?" "And do you not remember?" He says, "Do you not remember when I... broke the five loaves for the five thousand, how many baskets full of broken pieces you picked up?" They said, "Sure we remember, twelve." (Mk.8: 11-21)

"And when I broke the seven for the four thousand, how many large baskets full of broken pieces did you pick up? And they said to Him, 'Seven.' Do you remember? Do you remember a few weeks when I fed the five thousand men plus women and children, a crowd of 20 - 25 thousand? Sure, we remember the twelve baskets, one for each apostle. Do you remember the feeding of the four thousand?" By the way, in chapter 8 verses 1 through 8, that's immediately before this. It is sad how now we worry about the present problems and forget God's deliverance from similar issues in the past. The problems fill our minds and loom large like a great mountain, and we forget His promises.

3.3.4 Color Blind Christian

According to Rushton (1975), if just one pigment is missing, one might only have trouble seeing specific colors. On the other hand, if one does not have any pigments in one's cones, one will not see color at all, a medical condition called achromatopsia. Color blindness poses problems to people whose vocation involves color observation. For instance, drivers at the traffic light, chefs may need to know when a particular coloring is adequate,

---

[13] Eikenberry, K. (2008). Innovation Management. https://innovationmanagement.se/imtool-articles/eight-ways-to-generate-more-ideas-in-a-group/

laboratory technicians who need to see the endpoint in a titration of one compound against another, etc.

Cones control color vision. There are several kinds of pigments present in three types of cone cells. Some react to short-wavelength light, others to medium wavelengths and others to higher wavelengths. Revelations come in different ways. Those who are not used to God's different ways may lose out if He decides to speak in a particular way. God can shine His light on the scriptures for us to see the truth, but only as we put on all our wavelengths that revelation coming at a particular wavelength would not elude us.

The devil has introduced color blindness in the eyes of many believers that now see several issues from different perspectives, which subsequently affect their reactions and Christian living. When God restores a man's spiritual Sight fully, that man will undoubtedly avoid many mistakes in life. On the other hand, he will go astray quickly. The devil knows all these, that's why he colors people's perspectives to make them see things partially. Having a little knowledge of an issue, one takes an aspect and blows it out of proportion, thinking one knows it all or is doing the right thing. He gives a wrong interpretation of the scriptures and, of course, misapplies it. Consequently, he does not achieve anything and then begins to doubt the efficacy of the Word of God.

CHAPTER FOUR

GOD'S WAYS OF BLESSING HIS CHILDREN

4.1 Introduction

Revelation is essential for obtaining solutions to several issues of life that affect individuals, communities, a state, and a whole nation. My prayer is always that God will open my eyes to see. I believe you will also make it your prayer when you realize that there are things you need to understand in your life as a Christian. In Deuteronomy 8:18 (NIV), the Scripture says, "*But remember the LORD your God, for it is he who gives you the ability to produce wealth, and so confirms his covenant, which he swore to your ancestors, as it is today."* God gives us skills and unique talents that we use in our businesses. He provides us with the ability to make money and cut deals. He did it for others; he will do it for us too.

In 2 Corinthians 9:8 NIV, Paul wrote, *"And God can bless you abundantly, so that in all things at all times, having all that you need, you will abound in every good work."* God always delivers to us what we need in order to do our best work. "For I know the plan I have for you," declares the Lord (Jeremiah 29: 11 – 13). He plans to prosper you and not harm you; he plans to give you hope and a future.

Generally, there are some ways revealed in the Scripture that God blesses his children and enriches them. Here are some of them.

4.2 Existence of a Problem

Several examples in the Old Testament illustrate how God blesses His children. The first thing God does is reveal a problem to a king or someone in a position of authority. The revelation may be as simple as the man realizing that he should solve a particular problem in a nation's economy, education, sports, social life, and so on. Next, God can communicate to the King in a dream that no ordinary man can understand, like in the case of king Pharaoh and Emperor Nebuchadnezzar. In either case, God revealed to them some truths about their Kingdom but hid the actual interpretations from them. The dreams came with deep vexation and unrest, forcing each to seek for solution. They had no sleep. Their appetite for food vanished. God used the unrest in their minds to cause them to seek solutions. Like most of us, they had dreams before, some of which they forgot when they woke up; others they remembered. Generally, there are some dreams one cannot afford to overlook, especially when they look authentic.

In some cases, the dreamer wakes up with a start and sweat oozing out from his body. God constrains the dreamer to remember what he had dreamt and regard it to be very important. Then, He urges him to take action to understand its meaning. The dreamer narrates it to his friend or spouse and then prays about it, to come into fulfillment if it is a good one or never to manifest if it is a bad one. Some dreams may be so severe that the dreamer enters into an intensive prayer and fasting.

Pharaoh had a dream about Egypt and wanted an interpretation of it. His wise men and magicians were invited and couldn't give the interpretation. One of his servants suggested that they could consult Joseph. God revealed to Him the interpretation. His proffering a solution to it brought him recognition, honor, fame, wealth, riches, and promotion. His status changed overnight from an enslaved person to a prime minister, a pauper to a wealthy man. The correct interpretation brought him political influence, and he became Pharaoh's right-hand man.

It will not be wrong to say that God uses kings' pressing problems to bless His children.

In the case of Joseph, God was not only interested in teaching Pharaoh the economic lesson of food storage and preservation, but He also wanted to preserve the Jewish nation. These were His apparent aims. But there is a third one, though not apparent as the first two – He aimed at promoting Joseph. If it were not for this particular reason, to show He alone above all the gods of the Earth is omniscient and of infinite wisdom, and to reveal it to Joseph, He would have spoken to Pharaoh in clear language, in which case interpretation would have been unnecessary.

The case of Emperor Nebuchadnezzar is even more interesting (Daniel 2:1 -30). He had a dream by which his spirit was troubled and agitated, and his sleep went from him. The King couldn't remember the dream. He ordered the wise men within his Kingdom to reveal the dream and the interpretation; otherwise, destruction awaited them. He promised to honor and give wealth to the problem solver. The wise men were baffled. They replied that what he demanded from them was impossible. "... None except the gods can reveal it to the king and their dwelling is not with human" (Dan 2:11). The King was furious. He commanded that all the wise men of Babylon be destroyed. Daniel requested that the King should give him time to inquire from God. He met with his three Hebrew friends and prayed to God, who revealed the secret to him in a night vision. "... He gives wisdom to the wise and knowledge to those who have understanding. He reveals the deep and secret things: He knows what is in the darkness, and the light dwells with Him." (Dan. 2:21, 22 TABV; See also Job 15:8; Ps. 25:14; Mt. 6: 6)

Let us look at this issue critically. God gave the King a dream and made him very concerned about it. As far as the King was concerned, the dream was of utmost importance, and his wise men must interpret it. The King claimed he did not know the dream because we often forget our dreams when we wake up. Or he might be telling lies. Knowing how the so-called wise men would give all manner of interpretation to the dream, if he told them, he might have claimed he had forgotten it. His not telling the dream was to make sure he got the correct interpretation. We see here the omniscient God in action, the God who turns the heart of a king the way He likes.

Beyond the desire to ensure the correct interpretation, the King's action increased the degree of difficulty of the problem, and the bigger the problem, the greater the reward. Beyond God's intention to reveal Himself to the Gentile world, He also wanted to promote and bless Daniel. Compare Dan. 2:6 with Dan 2:48. The King had promised the person who revealed the dream and interpreted it gifts, rewards, and great honor. But the King gave Daniel many great gifts, set him ruler over the whole province of Babylon, and made him chief governor over all the wise men. Judging from the reactions of the wise men and the jealousy they exhibited, it is evident that if Nebuchadnezzar had promoted Daniel, no matter how much he liked him, it would have been difficult for Daniel to retain the position. God, the master planner, had to arrange a situation where a problem was created, competition existed and He revealed the solution to Daniel. Has God stopped using such means in our era? The answer is no. Jesus is the same yesterday, today, and forever. God is still revealing problems to His children. Call upon Him, as Daniel did, and He will show you great and mighty things you do not know.

It is worthy of note that both in the cases of Joseph and Daniel, it was the deployment of their gifts that brought them to the limelight. Yes, a man's gifts create opportunities for him and attract favor and honor. Where did you leave your gifts? Stop neglecting them and begin to apply them. Generally, God blesses His children in the following ways:

- Reveals solutions to economic, social, educational, and health problems
- Causes the inheritance of the wicked to be transferred to the righteous
- Stirs the ungodly to give to the righteous (favor)
- Directly multiplies the works of hands of the righteous (handwork and diligence)
- Through his gifts and talents
- Uses the creatures
- Uses other believers by speaking to them

4.3 Transfer of Wealth

God can also transfer the wealth of a whole nation to another country. This action enriches the country and the citizens of the benefitting country. During wars, he could do that if the benefitting country trusts in Him and invites Him to fight for her. A striking example was when three formidable armies of three countries attacked King Jehoshaphat of Judah. The land of Judah acquired many spoils from the war as God confused the attackers and instigated them to fight against themselves (2 Chr. 20: 1 - 25). Finally, God can also enable a believer to inherit the wealth of a wicked man by granting him special favor in the sight of the man or forcing him to relinquish it through other means.

In 1 Corinthians 2:16, the Scripture stated, "For who hath known the mind of the Lord, that he may instruct him? But we have the mind of Christ." We have the mind of Christ as our spiritual possession. The mind of Christ, with all its potential and potencies, is within us. The mind of Christ is full of the wisdom of God, and it is by wisdom that everything in this world was created (Proverb 8). There is untapped potential within every Christian to create things because of the mind of Christ that is full of the wisdom of God within them. One of the flows of the wisdom of God is to give knowledge of witty inventions. Proverb 8:12 says, "I wisdom dwell with prudence and knowledge of witty inventions." We often confess from Proverb 13:22 that the wicked stockpiles his wealth for the just. Could it be that such wealth (Pr. 13:22) is to come by creating wealth through innovation? Some may be waiting for someone to just dump money on them while God is ready to show us some new ideas that could create wealth. It could be on witty things: a new song; a new technology; a new phone app; an improvement to an existing product or process; an advancement in a method or device, and ideas that lead to a product or service that can solve a problem or satisfy a need.

4.4 Gifts and Talents

Every man has a gift. You have a gift, and if you are a Christian, the gift assumes greater significance. It is essential for achieving something worthwhile on Earth and for eternity. Have you identified the gifts and talents? Have you begun to develop them through exercise and application? If you have not, why not? God was not foolish when He imbued you with those gifts and talents. He did that to bless you. How wonderful and loving God is to put in you something special, something unique, something that makes you stand out among men. It is a special gift to you from God, and I am sure it is fantastic. The only problem is that you have overlooked it. You are searching for help elsewhere, outside yourself. Do you know that God does not do anything without a purpose? Sometimes we allow education, desire for wealth, the profession in vogue, parental advice, and so on to influence us to the point we only pay lip service to our talents and gifts or ignore them entirely.

Consequently, we grope about hopelessly and hop from one profession to another without achieving anything. How can you recognize your talent? Since your talent is what you came into the world with, it is usually what you enjoy doing. You find yourself deriving great joy doing it, and the results attract people's compliments.

Secondly, you do not need to be taught how to do it. Just a little effort brings terrific results. The fact is that people do not value what they have. Often, they will instead prefer to suffer or acquire knowledge in different areas and struggle to learn instead of developing the talents God has given them. Such people often do not have satisfaction with their job.

Although you can achieve some results as you use the talent in its raw state, you still need to develop it. It is like a natural diamond dug out from the Earth. It requires further polishing before it will shine, and everyone will appreciate its true worth. So also you need to polish your talents through study, education, and any other means available. God gave me the gift of writing, which I identified early in life. That gift helped me generate extra income for my family, even when we embarked on industrial action and the government didn't pay us for several months. Although I am a qualified engineer, I always enjoy writing – writing of all kinds.

I used to wonder why God gave at least a talent to everyman. First, it is a gift, a special birthday, or a conception gift. You and I never lobbied for it. He gave it to us irrespective of our color, tribe, nationality, religion, or political affiliation. It is a gift. As God's gift, it is unique. I don't think that the president of any country will give any of his subjects a worthless gift, needless to talk of God. God made us in His image. Because of His intense love, He sent His only begotten son to die for us. He appreciates us.

One usually gives a gift to express love and care. Besides, the quality of the present indicates the magnitude of love and closeness of the receiver to the giver. Since we are precious in God's eyes, His gifts to us can only be extraordinary.

4.5 Use of Other Creatures

God can do anything. With Him, all things are possible. He can use anything and anyone He likes to achieve His purpose. In the book of 1Kings 17: 4, 6, He used a raven to feed Elijah when he was troubled, depressed, and downcast. Our Lord Jesus was a believer in hard work. The Lord would have commanded the tax money to appear like a magician, but He never did that. At this time, many fraudsters are on a rampage with enticing advertisements that they could multiply money without work. So, our Lord had to send Peter to work to raise the money for His tax. God can use any creature to achieve His will for rescue operations in times of serious needs, but He has ordained that we should work. If you do not work, do not expect to eat. Work here is not just for salaried people. It is a generic term. It involves an effort to add value, such as parting with a gift, a talent, or a present or teaching, advising, counseling, involvement in production and marketing, etc.

So, stop wishing that money will appear in your wardrobe or pocket or a bag of rice in the kitchen when you are idle. Stop searching your pockets in your trousers for the money you did not keep, thinking God slipped a few notes in while you fritter away your time instead of putting your talents into use. Another way of creating wealth is through faith and belief in the Word of God. Believe His wonderful promises, and He will bring them to pass. He has already promised to bless you and make you wealthy. Our prayer is that He will open our eyes to understand what we should do to achieve His wonderful purposes for our lives.

    I once read about a girl who injured her leg after an accident. She needed to break an egg each day and spill the content around the wound. Her family was poor, and there was no egg in the neighborhood. The girl prayed to God for healing. She wondered where she would get the eggs. God could have done it by allowing the wound to heal miraculously. But He chose to use a hen. To everyone's surprise, a hen visited her house each day and laid an egg on a particular spot every day. God can speak to hens or any other creature to courier for Him.

CHAPTER FIVE

INNOVATION

5.1. Introduction

"Innovation is Christian when it is ultimately aligned with God's purposes and methods." - Gary W. Oster, *Christian Innovation Descending into the Abyss of Light*. Merriam-Webster defines the concept as introducing something new, like an idea, method, or device. Most people generally refer to innovation while speaking about technology or business. "Innovation—using our gifts and talents to bring about new ideas and way of thinking and working—is not just the preoccupation of a select group of thinkers outside the walls of the Church." Instead, innovation should be intricately woven into our spiritual lives in Christ. As Charles Spurgeon said, "To a man who lives unto God, nothing is secular, everything is sacred."

Although the Scripture did not use an exact word like innovation, it is packed with examples of innovation. "From God forming the Earth out of nothing (Genesis 1) to Solomon building the temple (1 Kings 6) and the counter-cultural lifestyle of the early Church (Acts 2) God has been calling his people to introduce new—often disruptive—ideas and ways of living for thousands of years."[14] When God created the world and man in His image and gave him rulership over all that he had created, Adam named the animals, manifesting his first act of creativity. God gave Adam and Eve the duty to

---

[14] https://www.bible.com/reading-plans/4553-discover-your-call-to-innovation/day/1

look after the garden. That work involved thinking, planning, and decision-making, all of which are aspects of the creative process.

After the fall, mankind's creativity continued in agriculture, building construction, forging tools, and music. Men began to practice the creative gifts that God had given them to fulfill his task of ruling over creation (see Gen. 4:20-21). God is the source of all creativity. And in creating man in his own image, he also gave man gifts of creativity. He gives these good and wonderful gifts to whomever He chooses (Ja. 1:17).

5.2 Definition

Innovation is a process that continuously builds on what came before it. Often, the best innovations are the ones that take previous ideas and find new ways to add value that the customers love.[15] Google defined it as "the action or process of innovating." The Oxford dictionary says it is making changes in something established, especially by introducing new methods, ideas, or products."

Skillicorn (2016) spoke to 15 of the world's leading innovation experts to get their definition of "innovation."[16]

The variety in their responses were:

"Innovation" is turning an idea into a solution that adds value from a customer's perspective. This requires a level of time and budget to take a rough idea, refine it, experiment on it, and finally turn it into a real solution – Nike Skillicorn

The application of ideas that are novel and useful. Creativity, the ability to generate novel and useful ideas, is the seed of innovation but unless it is applied and scaled it is still just an idea. – David Burkus

Innovation is about staying relevant. We are in a time of unprecedented change. Companies need to adapt and evolve to meet the ever-changing needs of their constituents- Stephen Shapiro

Innovation process: is a great idea, executed brilliantly, and communicated in a way that is both intuitive and fully celebrates the magic of the initial concept – Pete Fley

---

[15] https://www.ideatovalue.com/inno/nickskillicorn/2016/03/innovation-15-experts-share-innovation-definition/
[16] http://www.ideatovalue.com/inno/nickskillicorn/2016/03/innovation-15-experts-share-innovation-definition/

And The Lord Opened Her Eyes

Innovation is a feasible, relevant offering such as a product, service, process, or experience with a viable business model that is perceived as new and is adopted by customers – Gijs Van Wulfen

Introduction of new products and services that add value to the organization – Kelvin McFarthing

The fundamental way the company brings constant value to their customer's business or life and consequently their shareholders and stakeholders – Paul Hobcraft

Creativity is thinking of something new. Innovation is the implementation of something new – Paul Sloane

Innovation needs to be defined and agreed upon in each organization, making sure it is strategic, and everybody is aligned. Without it, misalignment results in less-than-optimal focus and results. As long as it includes "new" and it addresses customer needs and wants, any variation goes – Robert Brands

Innovation is work that delivers new goodness to new customers in new markets and does it in a way that radically improves the profitability equation – Mike Shipulski

Innovation is disobedience with a happy ending – Roberto Battaglia

Innovation is the implementation of creative ideas to generate value, usually through increased revenues, reduced costs, or both – Jeffrey Baumgartner

The use of innovation should be toned down – Stefan Lindegaard

Anything new, useful, and surprising. Great innovation is the simple ones that make you slap your forehead and say, "Gee, why didn't I think of that?" – Drew Boyd

New, organic value creation by applying creativity, in-depth relationships with consumers and customers, and new thinking – Michael Graber

Something new or different that delivers value to the world, with the key criteria that I am not innovating if I am not bettering people's lives. Put simply; it is the future delivered – Jorga Barba

Skillicorn analyzed the above definitions and found some underlying themes. The percentage of definitions that involve having an idea as an underlying theme is 60%; executing the idea, 60%; addresses a real challenge, 40%; adding value to the company, 40%; adding value to the customer, 40%; different perspective/thinking, 27%; and moving forward, 13%. While 13% showed definition is not important, only 7% indicated the importance of addressing the new market. From the results of the analysis, Skillicorn defined innovation as executing an idea that addresses a specific challenge and achieves value for both the company and the customer.

Innovation is related to creativity. Without creativity, there cannot be innovation. Creativity is to invent, to come up with a new way of presenting ideas, concepts, and useful things. The gift of creativity is the ability to use artistic skills such as art, drama, music, writing, dance, etc., for the glory of God and the edification of the church.[17] And so, when we think of creative gifts, we should not limit ourselves to just thinking about the creative arts – painting, sculpture, writing, music, dance, design, photography, and so on. All human endeavor involves creative gifts and abilities, from a simple setting of the table for dinner to the building of a vast cathedral.

5.3 Source of Our Creativity

God is the source of all creative gifts and innovation. God makes us creative like God. We have the mandate to look after the whole creation, which requires innovation. God breathed His life into us, imparting His likeness. And whenever we live into that likeness, whenever we heed the calling on our lives to steward, create, and innovate, that is when we most reflect our Creator. We are designed to be like Him, creating and innovating as we reflect Him to a world that has forgotten its Creator.[18]

When God created man, we read in Genesis 2:7(NIV): "The Lord God formed man from the dust of the ground and breathed the breath of life into his nostrils, and the man became a living being." That word "breathed" calls to mind God's spirit. So likewise, when you become a Christian, you become a new creation in Christ, "born of the Spirit" (John 3:8).

The Holy Spirit is part of all of God's creative acts, which implies God also gives us our creative gifts through the Holy Spirit.

In the beginning, God could have created the world at once, a perfectly working, complex system (Gen. 1). But He chose to innovate—each day adding intricately linked ecosystems and species that culminated in his most reflective creation: humanity. We are called to join Him in the ongoing innovative process of stewarding creation.

Innovation, the act that endows resources with a new capacity to create wealth, is the specific instrument of entrepreneurship. Equally, whatever changes the wealth-producing potential of already existing resources constitutes

---

[17] https://www.spiritgivengifts.com/creativity.html
[18] https://www.bible.com/reading-plans/4553-discover-your-call-to-innovation/day/2

innovation. Changing the yield of resources and the value and satisfaction obtained from them provides the opportunity for the new and different. Therefore, systematic innovation consists of the purposeful and organized search for changes in options that might offer economic or social advantages.

5.4 Purpose of creativity

God gives creative gifts for a purpose. Part of that purpose is simply for us to fulfill our role as human beings made in the image of God. A strong, biblically-based creational theology encourages us as Christians to get involved in all areas of life. Unfortunately, too often, we think of Christianity only in terms of the Bible, prayer, and other church activities.

Edify the Church

God does not waste His resources. Although He is God and can always replace, duplicate or produce things out of nothing, He does not like wastage. We saw that in Christ's attitude during the miracle of the feeding of the five thousand hungry people. The leftovers were gathered and not thrown away. So, God has given his gifts of creativity for a purpose. One of them is to beautify His bride.

Reflects God's Glory

We are to use all our gifts for God's glory and should not ignore any of them including the gifts of creativity (1 Tim. 4:14-15). Jeremy Myers said that there is nothing more needed in Christianity today than creativity. **Christianity must be creative because, first and foremost, we follow a creative God. The very first act of God recorded in Scripture is creation. Then, an eye-popping, universe-exploding, noisy, colorful cacophony of creative power unleashed into darkness and chaos.**

Effective deployment of our gifts can enable us to captivate people's imagination and inspire faith, challenge people's perspectives of God, and find fresh ways to convey the message and meaning of Christ's ministry. But we must always ascribe all glory to God. We participate with God in creation. Different people are given other gifts, but all are called to use creativity in developing their callings and carrying out their work.

The kind of rulership, dominion, or creativity we are to exercise is not to be something heavy-handed. On the contrary, Genesis 2:15 (NIV) indicates that humankind was placed in the Garden "to care for and keep" it, not to abuse it, but to develop a beautiful and productive garden. Creativity is our supernatural birthright. As the Heavenly Father creates, so shall His children. We are made in the image, bearing the God who built the universe out of the dust, with His innovation potential written into our DNA. (Saunders, 2015)

> *For the invention of the arts, and of other things which serve to the everyday use and convenience of life, is a gift from God by no means to be despised...as the experience of all ages teaches us how widely the rays of divine light have shone on unbelieving nations, for the benefit of the present life. We see at the current time that the excellent gifts of the Spirits are diffused throughout the whole human race. John Calvin's commentary on Genesis.*
>
> *Do not neglect the gift you have given you by prophecy when the council of elders laid their hands on you. – 1 Timothy 4:14*

Achieve God's purpose

Beyond the general overall purpose of reflecting the image of God in society by exercising your creative gifts, God also has some specific goals for the gifts he has given you. Going back to the tabernacle in Exodus 31, God had a particular purpose for the creative gifts he gave to Bezalel and Oholiab. The goal was to build a magnificent tabernacle with all the parts functioning well. "See, I have chosen Bezalel son of Uri, the son of Hur, of the tribe of Judah, and I have filled him with the Spirit of God, with skill, ability, and knowledge in all kinds of crafts." (Exodus 31:2-3)

"We are God's workmanship, created in Christ Jesus to do good works, which God prepared in advance for us to do" (Ephesians 2:10). Just as Bezalel and Oholiab produced quality workmanship for the tabernacle, you are the workmanship of Almighty God. And God has not only prepared specific works for you to do, but he also created you with the specific gifts necessary to do those good works. Make no mistake about it. God's gifts have a purpose, and God has a purpose for the creative gifts he has given you (Flowler, 2017; See also God's Gift of Creativity at http://www.rayfowler.org). Our Creator has given us creative energies and abilities that He wants us to use to help expand His Kingdom and righteousness. Many non-Christians think Christians are boring and stuck in their worn-out traditional ways of doing things. God gave Daniel extraordinary wisdom to be creative in the way that He overcame evil with good. The Lord wants to provide you with creative insight into all of your relationships, activities, and personal concerns if you let Him (Fritz, 2001)[19]

Demonstration of our Godlike Nature

God made the Earth by his power; he founded the world by his wisdom and stretched out the heavens by his understanding (Jer. 10:12). God applied His knowledge in creation when He formed the Earth and the heavens. Next, he created heaven, where His throne is, the mid-heavens, the astronomical heaven, and finally, the sky. He is creative. We manifest one of His fundamental attributes by being creative, which shows He is God and we are His children.

5.5 Benefits of Creativity

Just as with Bezalel, we are God's workmanship and were created to glorify God in good works. These works were "prepared beforehand" for us so "that we should walk in them" or so that we should do good things for Christ. We were created as His workmanship to be His working in the lives of others.

Recognition by God and Man

A man or woman who is skillful in his or her work will not go unnoticed by the Lord. To have a skill is one thing, but to use it in their work is altogether different, and God will notice those who have such creative skills, and they will be noticed by those in the world as well. Colossians 3:23-24 says, "Whatever you do, work heartily, as for the Lord and not for men, knowing that you will receive the inheritance as your reward from the Lord. This is because you are serving the Lord Christ."

We were created for work, and if we work heartily for the Lord and not for men, we will receive our reward. The word for "heartily" in Greek is "Ek" Psuches, 'out of the soul.' That is, it depends upon the effort that we put into it; therefore, the impetus is upon us to do whatever we are doing in life in a wholehearted effort.

In Ecclesiastes 9:10-11, the Scripture says, *"Whatever your hand finds to do, do it with your might, for there is no work or thought or knowledge or wisdom in Sheol, to which you are going."* This passage is similar to Colossians 3:23-24. *Therefore, we*

---

[19] https://www.sermoncentral.com/sermons/the-benefits-of-god-s-gift-of-creativity-paul-fritz-sermon-on-daniel-36616.

should do our work with zeal and strength to please God. In this life, only can we utilize our creativities for His glory because after we pass from this Earth, that opportunity will elude us.

Creates Opportunities for You

Your gift will make room for you and put you in the presence of great men.- Proverbs 18:16. Do you see someone skilled in their work? They will serve before kings; they will not serve before officials of low rank. (Prov. 22:29). God equipped us by giving us gifts at birth so that through training and education, we can develop and use them to create opportunities for ourselves, even where they do not exist. Joseph's dream, a special gift to God when He formed him in his mother's womb, raised him from the dungeon as a prisoner to the enviable, unique position of a prime minister in a foreign land.

Growth in Business Enterprise

Without creativity or innovation, Entrepreneurs struggle to survive. Entrepreneurs need to embrace the mindset of creative thinkers to come up with new ideas and solutions for important problems.[20] It is essential to acquire specific techniques for entrepreneurs to become better at the process of creative thinking and foster their creative genius.

Pitfall

God is the giver of all good gifts, so we should never take a wrongful pride in the talents and gifts he has given us. If we dare to usurp His position, the consequence will be disastrous (Agunwamba, 2008). "For I say, through the grace given to me, to everyone who is among you, not to think of himself more highly than he ought to believe, but to think soberly, as God has dealt with each one a measure of faith. As we have many members in one body, but all the members do not have the same function, we, being many, are one body in Christ and individually members of one another."

Having then gifts differing according to the grace that is given to us, let us use them: if prophecy, let us prophesy in proportion to our faith; or ministry, let us use it in our ministering; he who teaches, in teaching; he who exhorts, in exhortation; he who gives, with liberality; he who leads, with diligence; he who shows mercy, with cheerfulness.

---

[20] https://thepitcher.org/three-techniques-creative-thinkers-use-generating-innovative-ideas/

Let love be without hypocrisy. Abhor what is evil. Cling to what is good. Be kindly affectionate to one another with brotherly love, in honor giving preference to one another; not lagging in diligence, fervent in spirit, serving the Lord" (NKJV). Whatever gift we have should be viewed, used, and exercised with humility since we can do nothing without Him.

5.6 Examples of Creativity in the Scriptures

God can fill you with the skills to do all kinds of work. He has filled them with the skill to do all kinds of work as engravers, designers, embroiderers in blue, purple, and scarlet yarn and fine linen, and weavers—all of them skilled workers and designers (Ex. 35:31-32). God can also fill you with His creative spirit to achieve great things for Him.

We can use the gifts we have already or ask God to fill us with the spirit of creativity. Then the LORD said to Moses, "See, I have chosen Bezalel son of Uri, the son of Hur, of the tribe of Judah, and I have filled him with the Spirit of God, with wisdom, with understanding, with knowledge, and with all kinds of skills— to make artistic designs for work in gold, silver, and bronze, to cut and set stones, to work in wood, and to engage in all kinds of crafts. Moreover, I have appointed Oholiab, son of Ahisamak, of the tribe of Dan, to help him. Also, I have given all the skilled workers the ability to make everything I have commanded you."

Ephesians 2:10 stated, "For we are his workmanship, created in Christ Jesus for good works, which God prepared beforehand, that we should walk in them."

The Lord gave Daniel creative wisdom to demonstrate how godliness is profitable in all things. God showed everyone in the courts of Babylon how people who depend on Him for knowledge, understanding, and insight would prosper. As we fear God, He will fill us with wisdom and creative insight as He did to Daniel.

Too many people regret decisions that were hastily made by their appetites. We make good decisions when we are born again, and our minds are renewed to know God's good and perfect will concerning us. We can ask God to fill us with reverential fear of Him and propose to walk in His status in our hearts. Daniel and His friends showed creative wisdom as they chose to eat only vegetables they didn't sacrifice to idols, honored God by thanking Him for all provisions, and requested to be tested after ten days on a lean diet to express their dependence on God for their health. On the other hand, the other group chose to eat fatty foods, wine, and delicacies offered to idols for a blessing.

The fear of God caused him to be determined to please God, and God enriched him with His wisdom. That was how he could make the right decision. His choice to eat only vegetables was a wise decision that God revealed to him. He could have suggested other food which the officials offered to idols. But vegetables which in our times, many scientists have proven to be rich in minerals and nutrients and can refresh the skin and build up the immune system, unlike wine, while only might in the end left them dissipated, was the best. In addition to other advantages, vegetable has the unique characteristics of boosting rapid growth.

God may give us instructions just as He did to Adam and Eve in the Garden of Eden without telling us the details about how to do it. In such a case, it is our responsibility to use God-given thinking faculties to plan how to achieve the results. God wanted Adam and Eve to utilize their faculties in this endeavor. They were supposed to create structures. After all, He had made them in His image. If He were to do all for them, what would have been the use of giving them a mind or freedom to think or exercise their choice? In that case, it would be false to say they were created after God's image and consequently wrong to believe He even made the heavens and the Earth. If He had no free choice, then another person or force higher than Him propelled Him to create the heavens and the Earth. God forbid! God gave us the gift of creativity, and we should exercise it in all that we do.

5.7 God's Way of Giving Inspiration

5.7.1 Prayers

During creation, the Almighty Creator God stepped on the scene of a dark, desolate landscape and set it off with the marvelous light of the Kingdom. We should follow the same example of the Almighty when seemingly desperate situations confront us. As children imitating a loving Father, we should speak life into our problems.

Every time you want an idea, pray about it. God will open your spiritual eyes. Then, God can communicate with you through your creative spirit, and something will come through. God will always give an idea which is the key to all you want. So, a vision from God is all you need. With that idea, you can achieve great success.

You must, therefore, spend time in prayer until the visions come to your spirit and brood over those desires until you can speak the Word that will bring them to pass. When you say the Word upon that vision you received in your spirit, it becomes a reality but only in the spirit world. If you meditate upon these ideas long enough, they will become real to you, and your dreams will materialize as you pray about them. Bishop Oyedepo said, "You should meditate on the idea until it fills your thoughts and affect your confessions." Jesus Christ spent time praying, and every time He came down from the mountain, he performed tremendous miracles.

Ask Him

Take time to be alone with God. I have heard people say that God speaks to them when they are in the toilet or bathroom. He had also spoken sometimes when I was lying on the bed and meditating on His words. He spoke to me many times when I was taking my bath. I don't just understand why God will not talk only during quiet time. The Scripture reveals the Psalmist meditating on the Word and greatness of God as he lay on the bed receiving instructions from God.

When I thought about it, what came to mind was that God can speak to someone anywhere, by any means, and under any circumstance. God's ways are indeed mysterious. Therefore, our mind needs to be tuned attentively to Him always. We should not assume it is only in the church or place of worship that we can receive revelation.

Jacob, for example, received revelation about the angels in the bush when he was running away from home for fear of being killed by Esau after he cunningly received the latter's birthright blessings from Isaac, with the connivance of Rebecca.

The place and time were not conducive for meeting with God from the human point of view. Jacob must have been stressed out after a long journey away from home in a foreign land. Imagine the uncomfortable condition he was in. Fear of attack by marauders and wild animals lurking around in the bush must have gripped him. Emotionally, he must have suffered the trauma of leaving the comfort of home to find himself in an unfamiliar place.

Yet, God gave him a revelation and spoke to him. Does it then mean that we can receive revelation under any circumstance, place, and time? Yes. Does it mean we should live carelessly anyhow we want? No. Although he received revelation when he was not ready for it, the tiredness he felt and then sleep must have left him in a condition where his physical senses were subdued, and his subconscious exposed to receive from God.

In addition, he was alone. That is a critical condition to satisfy. We must try to be alone with God to receive revelation. Jacob was alone. Alone with God doesn't necessarily mean physical exclusion from others. One can be in the midst of many, and through meditation and attention to God, is temporarily detached from what is happening around him. However, that circumstance may not be optimal for receiving uninterrupted revelation since he could easily be distracted by the noise around him.

On the other hand, one could be physically alone in the church, bush, or wherever, and his mind is seething with anxiety about how to meet up with his needs and commitments. He is not emotionally detached from people and his needs. Under that circumstance, it is difficult to hear God speak to him. We must empty ourselves of all the junk about the cares of this world, activities, and commitments to receive from God. It is crucial, as much as possible to remove from our minds and around us every source of distraction so that our meditation on the Word will bear fruits.

God speaks more when we are alone with him. Think of several people God had ever spoken to or who had received one revelation or the other from God. God spoke to Abraham alone when He wanted him to leave his kindred, to offer Isaac, and under several different circumstances. The same with Isaac, Jacob, and Moses in the burning bush experience. Consider also the commissioning of Gideon, the man of courage. Remember David who knew much about God's greatness, omnipotence, and omniscience. His knowledge of God formed the bedrock of his faith, which manifested in the great faith he exhibited in destroying Goliath and subsequent victories against his enemies. His solid foundation was on the Word of God which he meditated on day and night, and absolute willingness never to rely on his wisdom but on God when he wanted to take any action. While alone in the bush as a shepherd boy, meditating on God's Word, he must have received many revelations that his warrior brothers did not know about.

Moses

God had to call Moses to the mountain several times where He spoke to him. There were cases where He talked to him when he was still with the people. God can still reveal things to us when we are with other people. But to receive the great and mighty revelations, like the ten commandments in the case of Moses, which may bring a significant turning point in our individual lives, we alone, not the pastor or counselor, may have to seek God.

As a jobless graduate for one year, as I waited on the Lord, he showed me that I would be a lecturer. It was a period of economic depression. Lecturers were languishing in hunger as their salary was extremely poor. Alone with God, He spoke to me. Despite the poor salary structure, I became a lecturer, despite opposition and advice from friends, my family members, and relations. The economic depression was so terrible that sometimes we lacked food. Shortly after that, the government improved the salary structure of lecturers. But it is always good to follow God's instructions no matter what we feel about it. The job has never been a bed of roses, but I have never regretted becoming a lecturer until now.

Mary, the Mother of Jesus

God spoke to her about the birth of Jesus. She was alone when the angel visited her. She was not even with Joseph, her betrothed, who sought later to put her away privately when he noticed she was pregnant. Why did God speak to her privately? Such a sensitive issue, for that matter! A problem that could bring her shame, contempt, and broken relationship? We must acknowledge that our ways and thoughts are different from God's.

As human beings, we would have reasoned that the angel speaking to both at the same time would have been better. That would have calmed Joseph over the situation. However, speaking to Mary alone sounds more reasonable in the light of what happened later when Joseph was planning to put her away secretly until he had a revelation himself. What a grievous mistake he would have made without a revelation! How sheepishly we sometimes act, following human reasoning because we do not understand the actual situation. We need revelation; just a word from God will settle our problems.

So, God did not reveal to Joseph at first. But why? Only God knows but let us try to explain. First, God deals with us as individuals. He speaks to us differently, even as spouses. In most cases, He talks to us individually on the same issue and tells the other person the same thing. Sometimes it happens simultaneously; at other times, there is a time lag. So, if your spouse is a believer, you can always get confirmation by employing this fact.

Another reason is that God does not ram His wish and opinion down our throats. He always speaks to us and elicits our willingness to obey Him. Notice that Mary wondered at the possibility of a virgin taking in and giving birth to a son. It was not possible from the human perspective. The angel's reply was, "that which is impossible with man is possible with God."

Why did God reveal this to Mary in the first place? After all, He is Almighty God. Why did He not go ahead and 'hijack' Mary's womb and do whatever He wanted? God would never do such. He is mighty, yet very considerate, kind, and loving. He goes out of His way to show His selfless love to us and waits patiently to win our love and trust, even when all these are for our good. Often, the lack of this wonderful attribute in us makes us use our minor privileged positions of authority in the church, government, and social circle to arrogate much power to ourselves and usurp other's rights to make freewill choices. Human beings will want to threaten you to subjection, whereas God would use sound logic that explains the benefits of His plans and clear all doubts. So, God solicited indirectly for Mary's co-operation.

Paul

God spoke to Paul while he was on his way to Damascus to persecute Christians in his usual way. But God arrested him and made him a defender and propagator of the Christian faith rather than the zealous prosecutor he was before. The men with him heard the voice he heard about his calling. God spoke to him publicly. He was a well-known persecutor who dealt seriously with the Christians. As his activities were public, so also his conversion so that his future ministry would never be in doubt. The witnesses he had during his spectacular conversion were to strengthen him and his ministry and the defense of the gospel several times.

Revelation does not mean we should not use our minds.

For some time, I used to frown at the men of God who heal the sick and proclaim the Word of God in faith and yet decide to attend church services and programs with a routine of police escorts and security officials. I used to denounce what seemed to me their hypocrisy and lack of faith in the Almighty God we serve. In my little mind, I used to reason that if these men could believe God to the extent of His using them to work miracles and wonders, why should they not also believe that the same God can offer them all-round protection anywhere, anytime under any circumstance? It was later that I began to fault my reasoning.

First, I tend to ignore that God deals with people as individuals. Experiential knowledge God shares with someone might be different from others, and people act based on the extent God has revealed Himself in specific areas. It is possible someone is used of God in an aspect of Christian ministry, yet he has not known Him as the chief security officer over his life and property. In such cases where a Christian is convinced to avail himself of the services of security men, he should do so because actually, that does not mean he does not trust God. He is simply using his God-given wisdom and resources to protect himself and ensure the Kingdom of God is advanced without hindrance. We can immediately consider the example of our Lord Jesus Christ in this regard.

He had retired to the seashore. A great multitude who had come from Galilee, Jerusalem, Idumea, and beyond Jordan, Tyre, and Sidon came to see him, having heard about His miracles. He told His disciples to have a little boat in constant readiness for Him because of the crowd, lest they press hard upon Him and crush Him.

Ponder on that verse. Jesus made plans against being crushed by the crowd. He was God and had all the powers. Off course, He could have disappeared and appeared if He wanted to at any moment. But I think this event showed how we should behave when a crowd, pressed by their selfish needs to receive healing or meet their other needs, is irate and unreasonable. The crowd would maim, kill or crush others to meet their needs. The Lord did not just let things be or rationalize. Since He had powers as God in the human flesh (like us, for as He was, so are we), He would have depended on miracles. God would deliver Him in every situation. He had promised to take charge of Him such that He would not kick His legs against a stone. It is always a problem to be balanced, know when to rely entirely on the Word for our healing, and go to the hospital when our faith is small, smaller than the mustard seed that could not make the mountain bulge. It is always a problem to know when to use our common sense to solve a problem or wait for revelation. If everything is to be solved by revelation, why did God give us the five senses? We must use them whenever we can and then rely on revelation when there is no revealed knowledge or information on the matter.

If our Lord planned ahead of time for his safety, to avert being crushed by the crowd, we too should make plans for our safety. We should hire security men if need be to guard ourselves and our property but still have absolute trust in God that He is the principal Security Officer. He neither sleeps nor slumbers and all the other security outfits are useless unless God is enthroned as the chief boss. "For even to this were you called (it is inseparable from your vocation). For Christ also suffered for you, leaving you (His personal) example, so that you should follow in His footsteps" (1 Pet. 2:21).

God loves to answer radical prayers. His Word is full of radical promises you can claim so you can see His radical answers. That was Saunders' experience. God opened her eyes to understand Jer. 33:3 as she prayed for a breakthrough in her life. Initially, she thought that God would do a miracle in her life. Then, she noticed that God did not say in Jeremiah 33:3 that He would DO tremendous and mighty things. Instead, He said He would SHOW us great and powerful things.

The Hebrew word here for "show" means to tell, make known, declare, announce, report, and inform of. She understood that God was talking about *telling* her new things she didn't know. He talked about conveying knowledge and ideas here and expanding our current reality. One of the things God showed her was very new ideas about her business.

Prov. 8:12 says, "I wisdom dwell with prudence, and find out knowledge of witty inventions." Prayer is important. If you want to bring God into your situation, you must pray. When you pray, something happens to you. Many people do not know how and why they should pray. You should depend on God for inspiration. Mark 11:24 says, "Therefore I tell you, whatever you ask in prayer, believe that you have received it, and it will be yours."

You will be surprised by God, who is very eager to answer your prayers. "Now to him who can do far more abundantly than all that we ask or think, according to the power at work within us, to him be glory in the church and in Christ Jesus throughout all generations, forever and ever. Amen" (Ephesians 3:20-21). Ideas are not necessarily restricted to professionals who are in the creative fields. You may be working as a clerk, housewife, or minister of God; you can still ask God to give you unique ideas.

Saunders, a businesswoman, started praying for God to show her the great and mighty things she did not know, things that would surprise her, and things impossible to anticipate. And God did it. She started getting inside information about things that matter to her- information to which she would not ordinarily have had access. Also, she started receiving radical ideas. Business ideas came to her out of nowhere.

Ask God for Daniel's Kind of Wisdom

James 3:17,18 says, "The wisdom from above is first of all pure (undefiled): then it is peace-loving, courteous (considerate), gentle, it is willing to yield to reason, full of compassion and good fruits; it is wholehearted and straightforward, impartial and sincere (free from doubts, wavering of insincerity). And the harvest of righteousness is the fruit of this seed sown in peace." Wisdom is the power to see and the inclination to choose the best and highest goal, together with the surest means of attaining it (Fritz, 2001).

This kind of creative wisdom brings peace, security, and fruit. It helps one make wise decisions without a trial-and-error method that often results in frustrations, disappointments, and discouragement. The good news is that we can ask God for wisdom. If any of you lacks wisdom, let him ask God who gives to all men generously and does not withhold (James 1:5).

It can even be as simple as creating a schedule to organize your day. We all can create something. When we are committed to doing things consistent with the way God designed human nature, we will flourish.

Stay-at-home mom, Gail Pittman turned an idea into a business venture. While looking for a creative outlet one day, she played around with ceramics and found joy in decorating pottery. She now has a company that produces ceramics and home décor employing over 110 workers.

Gail Pittman gives creative design and flares to the dinner table, turning the dullest kitchen into a work of art. Her company presents the business before God before making decisions and incorporates weekly Bible studies and practices that serve her community.

5.7.2 Believe

Can we trust God to give us creative ideas? The answer is yes. According to James 1:17(ESV), *"Whatever is good and perfect comes down to us from God our Father, who created all the lights in the heavens."* Also, Proverbs 18:15 (NLT) states, *"Intelligent people are always open to new ideas. They look for them."*

Believe that He who has called you is able to achieve results through you. Act in faith to bring that idea to fruition. Faith creates excellent minds with great ideas, and great strategies, always acting on them, while doubt sows in fear that makes one focus on impossibilities and insecurities. Focus on God instead of on yourself.

5.7.3 Act on the idea and do not be lazy.

Sadly, more often than not, we go around telling people about our God-given idea, but while they are still talking, someone else goes and invents it! God gives ideas so that we can profitably leverage them, with the end purpose being the expansion of His Kingdom, as simple as that!

Kin Kumar said, "I read about a man called Leroy Anderson whom God gave an idea to design a yo-yo with a light bulb inside. Although it seemed silly initially, nevertheless, he followed it, and today, Anderson owns the largest yo-yo company in North America! And can you imagine how much more he can support the Kingdom of God financially now than before?"

Mary Hunter, a housewife, based in Indiana, is the inventor of her patented Mary's Marinating stick. One day God gave her the idea to invent this cooking gadget called marinating stick (which looks sort of like a wide chopstick with holes). It eliminates the need to marinate the meat before the cooking process. Instead, while the meat is cooking, the natural juices of the meat help infuse the herbs and spices throughout, giving the meat a robust flavor. It took Mary Hunter 13 years to develop a prototype, and now her brand is a huge success!

"God does not show favoritism" (Acts 10:34). If God can give ideas to Anderson and Hunter, He can also give you. No matter who you are, you are creative no matter what you do. It is burned into your DNA. It is sealed on your soul (Andy Barlow, 2013). God has uniquely gifted you to leverage your creativity in this world for his glory and the good of others.

A Coach Develops New Sled

The man says, "I am a strength and conditioning coach, and one day while using sleds to condition my football team, I noticed that it was taking a long time for the team to turn the sleds once they got to the desired yard marker and then bring it back to the starting point. I was getting mad because it was a conditioning period, and it was not moving fast enough for my liking. I prayed later that night and asked the Lord to give me an idea of a better, more functional sled. He did! I am now working on a deal with a company to manufacture and sell it. I have also developed another piece of training equipment that will also be sold. I am also looking for people who have experience building apps because I have ideas for those."

A Postgraduate Student Finds New Doctorate research idea.

"God just gave me an idea for my research that would improve the academic scope of my project and make me an internationally sought-after innovator and generate greater ideas on biofuel production plant currently being developed in the United States. Yesterday, a professor challenged me and said my project was shallow. I did not take offense; I swung into prayers. Again, God gave me an idea."

Another person explained how God spontaneously gave him an invention that had passed the patent search with no prior art. The Lord led him to a business developer who is also a spirit-filled Christian and an inventor.[21]

"Did you know that God wants to give you amazing, wild, million-dollar ideas and witty inventions?" Rohrbaugh (2014) asked in his write-up titled "Wild ideas and Witty Inventions."

5.7.4 Create time to relax and think.

We need rest for our system to operate at optimum from time to time. That is the way God has designed it. The more we relax and think deeply about the issues of life, the more we generate ideas. We shall deal with this aspect in a subsequent section.

Sarah discussed how God inspired some inventors to invent. They listened to the creative unction of the Holy Spirit and branched out on ideas that the Lord placed in their hearts. We aren't, however, all creative in the same way. Some of us are ideators, gifted with the ability to pull new ideas out of nothing. Others are developers who add value to those ideas by turning them into something practical or workable. Then there are the creative visionaries who take those ideas and make them happen and evaluators who see a way of improving things that don't work so well.

She also said, "Some of us deeply feels the desire to create new things. We fill pages of notebooks with ideas for things we want to do or stories we want to tell. We dream of being published, exhibited, or having our ideas released upon the world somehow, not because of vanity or a quest for fame, but because the creative impulse within us yearns for satisfaction. For others, creativity feels elusive, like something that other people engage in. We'd love to get involved in the creative process, but we lack the confidence or some of the teachable skills that will allow us to do so. Whichever end of the spectrum you sit at, here are just a few ideas on how to approach the process of creativity and how to unlock your innate ability to innovate potentially."

5.8 Approaches for Unlocking our Potentials

5.8.1. Recognize that creativity comes from God

The Bible frequently reminds us of the incredible creative power of God. Jesus arrived on Earth not as a warrior King but as one of history's greatest storytellers. As was mentioned before, the story of the Bible started

---

[21] https://www.fromhispresence.com/prophetic-word-come-away-and-sit-with-me-awhile/

with the case of God creating the heavens and the Earth and making man in His creative image, which cannot be ignored.

5.8.2. Understand your creative role

Innovation begins as we recognize the problems and opportunities, then move through ideation, development, enhancement, piloting, release, and evaluation. Creativity is needed in every step of that process, and your skills, experience, and personality may make you most useful at one or two of those stages. If you can work out your link in the chain, you will be able to make yourself useful.

5.8.3. Feed your inner artisan

Sometimes we may run out of ideas. We can refill through prayers and by reading others' creative works. Film-makers are constantly watching other people's films; novelists are always reading. Not only does switching from output to input allow us to rest part of our brain for a while, but we often find that creativity is contagious.

5.8.4. Write it all down

Saunders said that Creative ideas sometimes strike us at the most inconvenient moments – the middle of the night, a cramped bus journey, or an important meeting halfway through the working day. Having a notebook on hand allows us to capture every half-idea to properly think it through later. This discipline of record-keeping pays dividends when, a few hours later, you can't remember a thing about that world-changing idea you had earlier.

5.8.5. Know your internal clock

The inner clock (also known as the circadian rhythms), an innate biological mechanism of the body, regulates its rhythmic and periodic cycles, including the feelings of sleepiness and wakefulness. It turns out that the same genes and biological factors that govern our internal clock are also involved in how other body systems operate -- and break down. Keeping the body's daily cycle on an even keel may be one of the best things for your overall health. A very distinct brain region called the suprachiasmatic nucleus (or SCN), which is situated right above the point in the brain where the optic nerve fibers cross is charged with keeping time. Its location enables it to receive the cues it needs from light in the environment to help it keep time.

The biological clock can be disrupted in certain people by aging, the quantity of light admitted into the eye, genetic predisposition, and lifestyle choices, such as alcohol consumption, jet lag (air travel), or shift work. Science continues to discover meaningful connections between a disrupted clock and chronic health issues, from diabetes to heart disease to cognitive decline. In addition, disrupting our body's natural cycles can cause problems such as frequent traffic accidents and workplace injuries when we spring forward loss of an hour of sleep (Walton, 2012), and reduced fertility (Klein, 2014).

But keeping your schedule on track as much as possible is probably the best advice. **Camping could help reset it to a more natural rhythm** (Klein, 2014). Avoid disruptions to your eat-sleep cycles. Practice good sleep hygiene, and stick to a sleep schedule that works well for your body to keep the system in its natural rhythm. Turning in a little earlier, cutting back on caffeine late in the day, and saving that last bit of work for the morning rather than staying late up to finish it, can make a big difference in how your internal clock functions and how you feel (Walton, 2012).

5.9. Ways of Getting Inspired Ideas

5.9.1 Direct Revelation from God

As the Heavenly Father creates, so shall His children. Here are the five inventions based on God's inspired ideas[22]:

Peanut Products

As a science enthusiast, George Washington Carver once asked God to tell him the universe's secrets, but instead, God pointed him to something much smaller – the peanut.

The secrets Carver discovered led to hundreds of discoveries including peanut butter, cosmetics, paint, oil, marble, plywood, and even the dye used in Crayola Crayons. Carver, humbly attributing all of his inventions to the Creator, has often said, "The Lord has guided me," and "without my Savior, I am nothing."

---

[22] https://www.beliefnet.com/inspiration/galleries/5-inventions-that-were-god-inspired-ideas)

Laser Printer

Gary Starkweather, the inventor of the laser printer, encourages believers to think biblically about their work. As an engineer and inventor, he worked with leading technology innovators, such as Apple, Microsoft, and Xerox. However, he credits the success of his inventions to the guidance and inspiration of God. "I believe that to a great extent, the creativity we possess is because the Creator puts it there," says Starkweather. "God puts things [in us] as tool developers and creative individuals, and I think it has to please him when He sees us use those faculties to make something completely new."

Tyndale Translation Bible

Theologian and scholar William Tyndale invented the first English Bible translation to work directly from the original texts and be more easily understood by the general public. The Catholic church did not well receive Tyndale's Bible translation and in fact, they accused him of heresy. However, Tyndale was committed to reforming the church and making the Word of God accessible to more people. This, unfortunately, meant losing his life for the cause the Lord gave him. Today his translation influenced many of the English Bibles that have shaped millions of Christian lives worldwide.

Marinating Stick

Award-winning chef, Mary Hunter, tells the New York Times that all her recipes are divinely inspired, "I don't have a cookbook," she said. God gives me my own. Prayer is "where I get 99 percent of my recipes." One day Hunter says God gave her an out-of-the-box idea: a marinating stick that outperforms herbal injectors restaurants typically resort to. Although the idea took time to come to fruition, it was first given in 1994 and took nearly two decades to make its way into the stores – it was worth the perseverance.

5.9.2 Dreams

Many of society's innovations have come from dreams, proving that sometimes there is a method in our brain's madness. God revealed to some inventors some inventive ideas in dreams. They listened to the creative unction of the Holy Spirit and branched out on ideas that The Lord placed in their heart. Creativity is our supernatural birthright. God can also use dreams to speak to people about inventions.

The Sewing Machine.

In 1845, Howe was desperately trying to work through technical problems with his invention, but he kept running into an infuriating brick wall when it came to the design of the needle. Well, according to members of his family, it finally all came to him in the course of a ludicrously violent and somewhat racist nightmare. In the dream, he had been captured by cannibals. As is typical of bloodthirsty natives, Howe's captors presented him with an ultimatum - come up with a design for a working sewing machine, or face death. Just like in real life, he failed to live up to the task, and so the cannibals sentenced him to be stabbed to death with spears. Hey, this was the 1800s -- at the time, like every third person died this way. The remaining two people choked to death on their beards.

He noticed that each spear had a hole in the tip. Watching them puncture his flesh, going in and out, was allegedly the "Eureka!" moment that led to Howe figuring out that he needed to put a hole in the tip of the needle in his sewing machine. The device worked, and Howe died a rich man.

James Cameron Dreams the Terminator

In 1981, director James Cameron was pretty much unknown in Hollywood. His greatest accomplishment at that time was *Piranha II: The Spawning*, a cautionary tale about genetically engineered flying carnivorous fish. Cameron, of course, had greater ambitions beyond flying piranhas. He desired to make an action movie reminiscent of the old *Outer Limits* episodes he watched as a kid. He just didn't know what to write about. But while he was in Rome working on the post-production of *Piranha II*, Cameron grew sick and had to leave early to go to bed. That night, he had a fever dream -- there was an explosion, and coming out of it was a robot, cut in half, armed with kitchen knives, crawling toward a fleeing girl. Despite a 102-degree fever, Cameron sketched the robot down after he awoke, and once back in the United States, he hammered out a draft of what would become *The Terminator*. The finished product was a hit, and it was Cameron's first step toward becoming one of the biggest names in Hollywood.

Special Theory of Relativity

According to David De Lossy in Digital Vision/Getty Images, it was said that Einstein dreamed that he was walking through a farm when he came upon a bunch of cows huddled up against an electric fence. The farmer suddenly switched the fence on because apparently, he was that much of an asshole, and Einstein watched all of the cows jump back at the same time as they got shocked. Assuming that he had witnessed some kind of synchronized cow acrobatics, Einstein recounted what he had seen to the farmer, standing at the opposite end of the field. But what the farmer had seen was different – he had seen the cows jump away one by one like they were doing the wave at a football game. This would have been hilarious, and one assumes this is why he did it. After meditating on the problem for a while, he started to put together the idea that events look different depending on where one is standing because it takes time for the light to reach one's eyes. That was the birth of the theory of relativity.

A Scientist Dreams of Snakes, Discovers Benzene

Benzene revolutionized the production of things like cars, rubber, fuel, leather clothing, and other items. Serving as a primary component of explosives during World War I, it was used for everything. In the mid-1800, Friedrich August Kekule von Stradonitz discovered the founding principles of its chemical structure. For several years, scientists had been trying to crack benzene's molecular structure because, again, they were pretty sure it could change the world. However, every configuration of molecules that they tried didn't work for a variety of scientific reasons, a problem that Kekule soon ran into during his experiments. That is until he had help from a dream about frustrating snakes.

Exhausted from having every avenue of inquiry ironically hampered by the laws of chemical structure that he had invented years earlier, Kekule decided to have himself a fireside nap. Once asleep, he had a dream in which he was surrounded by snakes that formed themselves into hexagons, which he realized upon waking was the shape of the benzene molecule he was trying desperately to crack. Legend has it that after Kekule woke up, he worked through the night to successfully recreate what he had witnessed, presumably spending the whole time trying to tie a bunch of garden snakes together. Or maybe he just did not want to fall asleep and have more snake nightmares. Either way, it worked.[23]

---

[23] Ryan McVay /Photodisc/Getty Images/Jupiterimages/Photos.com/Getty Images

Descartes' Crazy Dream Creates the Scientific Method

Rene Descartes, the man who originated the Cartesian coordinate system, had a dream[24] where he found himself caught inside a vicious whirlwind and been pursued by a group of ghosts. Descartes had to wait in a ghost-filled melon-craving purgatory until the wind died down, and he was taken into a room that kept trying to set him on fire with red-hot sparks and deafen him with near-constant thunderclaps. Somehow, he escaped and found himself inside a peaceful, still room with only a book for a company (this is still in the dream, mind you). Descartes opened the book and read a single line: *"Quod vitae sectabor iter"* ("What path shall I take in life?"). Then a man appeared next to him and spoke *"Est et non"* ("Yes and no"). The man and the book then disappeared, leaving Descartes to think about how utterly unhelpful that answer was.[25] But Descartes believed that God communicated the dream to him and that he knew what it meant: that he was to try to reinvent the way humans think about the universe. Consequently, he went on a pilgrimage and dedicated the rest of his life to figuring out science principles. That was how he developed the principles of science.

The summary of some of the inventions through dreams is as follows:

- Mendeleyev created the periodic table from a dream.
- Frederick A. von Kekule solved the structural riddle of the benzene molecule (a closed carbon ring) from a dream in which he saw a snake seizing its tail.
- Frederick Banting isolated insulin with help from his dream.
- Elias Howe finished his lock-stitch sewing machine from a dream.
- The inventor of the compound bow received the idea for the invention in a dream.
- a dream inspired Einstein's theory of relativity.
- Through a dream Handel received the last movement of Handel's Messiah.

God is full of good ideas, and He loves to give His people witty inventions.

---

[24] Hemera Technologies / AbleStock.com / Thinkstock / Comstock / Getty Images
[25] https://www.cracked.com/article_20498_5-famous-things-you-wont-believe-were-invented-in-dreams.html

5.9.3 Analysis of Human System

By studying the human system and how it functions, man can mimic the marvelous handiwork of God and pattern his after God. For instance, scientists and engineers have designed and built wastewater treatment plants by studying osmosis in human bodies and leaves. A friend of mine, a microbiologist, explained how he would generate energy by mimicking the processes whereby plants generate their own.

5.9.4 Other God's Creature

Pondering over the rich, awe-inspiring, and wondrous works God has made is always a source of generating great ideas. Pause and think about the trillions upon trillions of stars, so far apart that it would take one millions of years to travel from one end to the other at the speed of light. And our Earth is delicately balanced on its axis, tilted at 23½ degrees so that we get the four seasons; winter, spring, summer, and autumn. Consider the incredible variety of beetle on the planet, three hundred and sixty thousand different beetles. Tress, fish, and six billion human beings, yet no two are the same.

One of the people's most significant sources of inspiration is nature, wrote Arrington (2011). When we experience a beautiful view, watch animals or hike a mountain trail, it inspires us. The creative part of our brains can get turbo-charged in God's creation.

But God also speaks to us in unlikely places. He can inspire us with ideas that use our talents no matter where we are. She recounted that George Frideric Handel was a German musician and composer. The rulers of England paid him to compose music for celebrations, musical productions, and worship. One of Handel's most famous works, Messiah, is about the life of Christ and includes an orchestra, choir, and solos. Handel wrote Messiah in just 24 days during the summer of 1741, alone in a room. A servant overheard Handel say, "I did think I did see all heaven before me and the great God himself." So, when we hear the "Hallelujah Chorus," we can also feel like we're getting a glimpse of heaven.

The ideas that could result from studying the behavior patterns and nature of birds of the air, aquatic living organisms, and animals are inexhaustible. God has not only created them of different species but also with different unique characteristics that can furnish one with a unique insight and innovative ideas. Some years back, some people started wondering why and how a specific plant named 'touch and die' closes its leaves and shrivels temporarily when touched by an object and then recovers after a few seconds. Findings showed that it was due to electrical charges in the leaves. Scientists had long ago started investigating if they could harness the charges in reasonable quantity for an economical supply of electricity. Apart from God's desire to display His manifold wisdom by creating such a wonderful plant imbued with charges, He might have also provided alternatives to fossil fuel. According to Bennett (2008), plants inspired the following inventions:

Velcro
Velcro is a fastener found on bags, children's shoes, and astronaut suits. The sticky material was inspired by how plant burrs stick to dog hair or fabrics. Swiss engineer, George de Mestral, observed the plant as it latched on nimbly to his dog and his pants after a hunting trip in the Alps in 1941. He found that the tiny hooks allowed them to stick to things with loops and thought it could be replicated into something useful. So, after years of experimentation, he invented Velcro, the zipperless-zipper. He earned a patent for the invention in September 1955. Velcro is known today as a brand of fabric hook and loop fasteners.

Bullet train
Bullet trains are named that way since they are designed to mimic bullets. These high-speed trains were successful, but they had one persisting problem. As the train drives through, air pressure builds up in waves, causing a shotgun-like thunderclap sound when the nose emerges. Passengers experience headaches and feel that the train is squeezing together whenever it exits a tunnel.

Eiji Nakatsu, an engineer at the Japanese rail company JR-West, was an avid birdwatcher. He observed that the kingfisher, a fish-eating diver bird, has long beaks that cut through the air and barely make a ripple when they penetrate the water. So, he decided to apply the structure of the kingfisher's beak to the front of the trains, which did not only help the train to exit quietly out of tunnels but permitted faster speeds and increased energy efficiency. The Shinkansen bullet train in Japan has a maximum operating speed of 320 km/h and produces only around 16% carbon dioxide of the equivalent journey by car. It is a type of nose job that made a huge difference.

Stronger but gentler medical tape

Spider silk is one of the strongest materials in nature, being five times stronger than steel by weight. It is also stretchy and sticky – but not sticky in other places so that the spider can dash across it. Scientists mimicked that property when they had an idea that they can apply to medical adhesives. Ripping off Band-aids and most medical adhesive tapes can sting a bit, but it can be painful and damaging for the sensitive skin of newborns and the elderly.

They created a flexible silk-inspired adhesive tape that can be peeled off without damaging the skin tissue underneath. Scientists applied a silicon-based film to the backing material and then used a laser to engrave a grid pattern on the silicon. This tape helps attach tubes or sensors to patients' delicate skins.

Anti-fouling coating for ships

Unlike other marine creatures, Sharks stay squeaky clean for more than 100 million years. As a result, they don't collect slime, barnacles, or algae on their bodies. This intrigued an engineer named Tony Brennan, trying to make a better coating for US Navy ships when he observed it in 2003. Barnacles and other sea organisms create extra weight and cause drag on the boat, reducing fuel efficiency and causing the Navy to spend at least $50 million a year to remove them from ship hulls. He discovered that the shark's tiny, tooth-like scales prevented organisms from glomming on their skins (or biofouling).

Brennan's observation led to the development of Sharklet, a synthetic shark skin material that has the same anti-biofouling attributes and is manufactured by Sharklet Technologies. It has shown positive results in inhibiting marine growth on the surface of ships. German researchers also developed the same material made of elastic silicone, and it has been proven to reduce biofouling by 67%.

Antibacterial medical devices

The unique property of shark skin did not only benefit the shipping industry – the medical industry and the ordinary people could take advantage of this development. Scientists have examined that shark skin-like material can prevent the growth and spread of disease-causing bacteria such as E. coli and Methicillin-resistant Staphylococcus aureus. It is good news for the healthcare sector since bacteria and viruses still spread even in hospitals whose nurses and doctors constantly wash their hands.

And The Lord Opened Her Eyes

Since the catheter is the most frequent transmitter of hospital-acquired infections, Sharklet Technologies have integrated its shark skin-like technology into the medical device and other hospital tubes and wound dressings.

Brighter LED lights

You are probably familiar with light-emitting diodes (LEDs), they are more energy-efficient than incandescent and compact fluorescent bulbs. But much of the light LEDs produce remains trapped in their inner surfaces. So, scientists found inspiration in the twinkling fireflies to modify the outer coating of LED bulbs. They studied the internal structure of the firefly lanterns and identified an unexpected pattern of jagged scales, which prevented reflection and enhanced the glow of the firefly's light. Researchers have applied this knowledge to build a brighter LED design. Their creation made the bulbs emit one and a half times their normal light.

Cheaper solar cells

The usual way of making solar cells uses techniques that use tons of energy, toxic chemicals, and expensive materials and processes. But the humble, orange puffball sponge does it better than humans since they simply release enzymes into the water, pull out the silicon and calcium, and then arrange these chemicals into specific shapes.

Daniel Morse, a molecular biochemist, a professor, and his colleagues, discovered this superb ability of the sponge. They studied its enzyme technique and tried to copy its mechanism. In 2006, they created electrodes that use clean and efficient sponge technology. Thanks to this sponge development, we are now experiencing an era where solar power is cheaper than fossil fuels.

Better water filter

For a long time, it has been known that there must be pores in a cell membrane for water and salts to flow in and out of cells. After careful consideration of this theory, scientists discovered that there must be a selective filter that prevents ions from passing since only water molecules can flow freely. It has been a long-standing mystery in biochemistry, and it was only solved in the 1990s when biologist Peter Agre discovered Aquaporin, a membrane protein that allows such phenomena. Aquaporin molecules happen to maintain osmoregulation in living organisms. Agre received a Nobel Prize in 2003 due to this discovery.

For the past several years, many studies have been made to utilize Aquaporins, or replicate their functionality, to develop a more effective alternative to existing water purification techniques that use less energy. One company, Aquaporin, has developed water treatment technologies that integrate essential aquaporin proteins to restrict the passage of contaminants including bacteria, viruses, DNA, dissolved gases, and even protons without hindering the passage of water. The company applies it in commercial products like industrial water and wastewater streams treatment and other segments.

Skin graft adhesive

Think all worms are just parasites? They can serve as a scientific inspiration, too. For example, a new surgical technique for skin grafts – transplants to treat wounds or burns – is based on a parasitic, spiny-headed worm, *Pomphorhynchus laevis*. This worm pierces the intestines of its host with its razor-like spine and then bloats its cactus-like head inside the tissue to stay attached.

Researchers mimicked this mechanism to create patches of tiny, cone-shaped needles whose tips inflate when exposed to water, keeping the graft in place. The needles would pierce the tissues with minimal force and pressure to the tissue. After removing the adhesive, the skin transplant would cause less trauma to the tissue and nerves than skin staples and sutures commonly used by surgeons. It would also carry a significantly smaller risk of infections.

Colored e-reader display

Qualcomm, a manufacturer of processors and chip components used in smartphones and tablets, is enjoying tremendous success in the mobile industry. Besides their processors, Qualcomm was also known for successfully creating the first full-color, video-friendly e-reader prototype. They have built their concept on the iridescence of a butterfly's wing and adopted the mechanics into the technology, making it a better alternative to LCD screens.

The display by Qualcomm, which they named Mirasol, provides better visibility in bright sunlight. Like a butterfly, its reflective displays can be easily seen even in bright light. Mirasol displays also need no backlighting, resulting in lesser energy consumption and longer battery life. Without the need for backlighting, this paved the way for thinner e-readers and thinner cell phones, gaming devices, and digital cameras during the 2000s.[26]

In addition to the above cases, five plants, often with a green lining, with surprising superpowers, have provided a boost to technological innovation or invention.

Algae and Biofuel

Algae can be eaten, burned for heat, or used to produce hydrogen, methane, biodiesel, or plain old fertilizer. Algae are so prolific and come in so many varieties that it is a chore to isolate your preferred species for cultivation out of a water sample from the wild. The best part is that algae soak up the sun and lots of carbon dioxide to work their magic. Two forms of renewable energy are used to produce fuels or foods in high demand. An alga culture biodiesel plant is already in operation today, happily churning out 4.4 million gallons of algal oil per year. That may sound small, but as the first operational algae oil factory, they can make enough money to build bigger ones. Other companies are also in the game to make algae the most significant thing after oil. As a renewable source of fuel, algae are becoming one of many solutions to our energy problems. Not too shabby for pond scum.

The discovery of algae's potential is quite significant. Politicians seem dead set on promoting biodiesel as the fuel of the future. Even if this trend gives way to electric automobiles, there's still going to be a significant demand for biodiesel to run larger engines. We have all read about the problems with land-cropped biofuels, including pushing out food production and harming the environment. Algae is great because it avoids both of these consequences. But perhaps the best thing about algae is its fantastic efficiency. One acre of algae can produce 10,000 gallons of biodiesel in a year, compared with 20-50 gallons per acre for crops like corn and soy (Dube, 2007)

Guayule and Latex

Guayule is a desert plant native to North America. One company, Yulex Corp., realized that this little plant had a lot to offer. Guayule can produce rubber, unlike production from most natural rubber, which leaves the crop at risk from the disease. Latex made from guayule performs better than traditional latex, and it is allergy-free. Softer, stretchier, firmer, and an effective barrier – Yulex latex products are already on the market and in high demand

---

[26] https://didyouknowscience.com/amazing-inventions-inspired-by-animals-and-plants/

from the medical, scientific, and contraceptive sectors. Latex gloves might not seem like a huge technological breakthrough.

Guayule also produces resin, an ingredient in everything from paint and paper to particle board and soap. Scientists are also trying to make lumber products (think plywood) from it, and they hope to use what is left over to produce bio-energy and ethanol. Because guayule is a hearty desert crop, it requires little water or fertilizer to grow. As a result, the plant has a high energy content, making it attractive for upcoming cellulosic ethanol and syngas technologies. Farmers can use similar methods and machinery from cotton fields to grow and harvest guayule, making the switch easy.

Corn and Plastic

Interestingly, one can make more than high fructose syrup from corn. Starches are used in everything from paper to detergent, and dextrose gives us everything from antibiotics to wine. You can even make tires out of corn. A favorite use for corn is plastic: biodegradable corn plastic. The problem with most plastics is that it never goes away; it just breaks up into tiny pieces forever. It kills animals, and in some parts of the ocean, there are almost as many plastic granules as sand.

Biodegradable plastic provides benefits without ecological damage or a petrochemical base. Even though corn gets a bad rap these days (for some good reasons), one would rather have a renewable plastic source that will break down eventually. Remember that plastic provides us with everything from medical equipment to computer cases. Many cutting-edge technologies depend on it, but that does not mean we want it around forever. That's why this innovation made the list.[27]

Lotus Plant and Nanotechnology

The lotus plant grows in muddy waters, but its leaves emerge clean. This is because the leaves are not smooth, yet water rolls off of them and collects dirt along the way. This phenomenon is called the Lotus Effect. Microscopic structures on the leaf trap air bubbles and repel moisture with a waxy coating. The result is droplets of water dancing on tiny spikes instead of a flat surface. Since there's nothing to cling to, the water is forced to roll away on the slightest decline. This superhydrophobic coating is excellent against water droplets, but it doesn't work well against water vapor.

---

[27] https://cleantechnica.com/2008/08/04/top-5-plants-that-inspire-new-technology/

The applications for water repellent and self-cleaning coatings are almost unlimited. Imagine tools and surfaces that bacteria, food, and dirt cannot stick to. Imagine clothes that rarely need to be washed. These coatings already exist, and some are on the market. It can also be made with safer or fewer chemicals and increase the life cycle of many materials and resources.

The lotus plant has been a symbol of purity in Asia for thousands of years, in part thanks to its superhydrophobic leaves. Understanding how and why are perhaps just as enlightening as observing the phenomenon, as they offer insight into the ingenuity of evolution and natural systems.[28]

5.9.6 Man's Creation

A diligent study of man's designs, construction, and systems will reveal imperfections. Then, someone could critique the different deficiencies and find how to remedy the shortcomings.[29]

One of the ways God manifests Himself is by giving His people witty inventions. Likewise, God gives gifts to men and women, such as creativity. Our Creator has endowed us with specialties in differing areas, just as He has given each member of the Body of Christ gifts of the Spirit (Wellman, 2015). History is full of inventions God downloaded to men and women through dreams, visions, and just plain wild ideas. Examples of such dreams are (Rohrbaugh, 2014):

God gave Bezalel extraordinary abilities and talents to work creatively on the construction of the tabernacle of God. These creative abilities included intelligence, knowledge, and skill in his craft. God expected Bezalel to pass along these abilities, so He "inspired him to teach, both him and Oholiab, the son of Ahisamach of the tribe of Dan. He had filled them with the skill to do every sort of work done by an engraver or by a designer or by an embroiderer in blue and purple and scarlet yarns and fine twined linen, or by a weaver—by any sort of workman or skilled designer" (Ex 35:34-35). The Lord gave Bezalel these creative gifts and expected him to teach these skills to others (Ex 35:34-35).

---

[28] https://steemit.com/science/@kendoonpoint/impressive-inventions-inspired-by-plants-and-animals-762a201deb021
[29] http//:www.cracked.com/article_20498_5-famous-things-you-wont-believe-were-invented-in-dreams.html

CHAPTER SIX

GENERATION OF IDEAS USING HUMAN TECHNIQUES

6.1 Introduction

There are various ways humans try to generate ideas. God has given the human mind to think out good ideas. God equally created the mind, and with it, Adam was able to name the animals, birds, and other living organisms. Whatever he named each became its name. God never changed that because He delegated that function to him. God involved a man in certain aspects of the creative processes. Making Adam and Eve in His image, He automatically imbued the power of creativity in them. A man can create like God if he renews constantly; otherwise, he can employ the mind to think out the evil that might threaten man's very existence. This has been replayed in history frequently in the proliferation of weapons of mass destruction as nations jostle for power supremacy. Knowing that, man has continued to perfect the process of generating ideas through thinking. Although some of the ideas resulting from such procedures are evil, it does not mean the techniques are wrong. It only underscores the tendency of man to indulge in evil if he does not control his mind. It also shows the depravity of ideas generated when God, the giver of every good and perfect gift, is shut out from the human mind. When God is not central, man's "thoughts will continually be evil." However, some of the methods of generating ideas are discussed in the subsequent section.

6.1.1 Rules of Brainstorming (Alex Osborn's Applied Imagination)

Multiple people can generate ideas in parallel instead of in sequence. A group should create ideas together by allowing one person to speak at a time. The others should listen and then judge who will talk next. This means only one person can be active at any time. In contrast, all members can work and generate ideas simultaneously when working individually.

The brain cannot do convergent and divergent thinking simultaneously. Parents teach older children to immediately criticize ideas as they are developed. Since all ideas start imperfect, most people do not get past the initial hurdle and develop ideas further because people immediately reject them.

The first idea we hear contaminates our thinking. We react to external stimuli by giving them our focus to help us sense danger. Because of this, our brain is easily distracted, and hearing someone talk about our idea will require our brain to focus and prevent it from generating its own ideas.

We defer to authority. We intend to defer to more senior persons in the group and agree with their ideas because they are often experienced, and challenging them may be dangerous. This is why groups often accept the Highest Paid Person's Opinion (the HiPPO).

Loud extroverts may dominate the conversations. Consequently, more introverted persons may not contribute much.

We are afraid of having our ideas judged: Since our initial ideas are imperfect, many people are scared to let other people know about them because they will see all of the flaws in the idea and judge the idea and the person who proposed it.

We feel like we are all contributing, but this is an illusion.
There is a cognitive phenomenon called the *"Illusion of Productivity,"* where people think that during group brainstorming, they contributed more than they did and take credit for a disproportionately high amount of the ideas. In contrast, people do not experience these problems when they have time to write their ideas down first, instead of presenting them in front of the group. One can improve the Brainstorming session by giving individuals time to write down their ideas first before coming together to find commonality between everyone's ideas, assess the implications, and then refine and improve the best solutions. This technique is called *Brainwriting*. It helps groups generate more ideas and allows teams with individuals to work more effectively together.

6.2 Eight Ways To Generate More Ideas In A Group

It becomes easier to come up with great ideas when we free ourselves from the mundane, everyday, conventional thoughts that take up the thought space in our brain.[30] Group brainstorming is common in organizations around the world. Here are many ways to generate better ideas in these ideation sessions. One technique, however, will guarantee the perfect solution. Instead of your goals, one can adopt a combination of approaches to help stimulate idea creation in your repertoire. While doing this, one will improve the overall quality of ideas by having more to choose from. Given below are eight suggestions that could help. Eikenberry (2008) discussed eight ways of generating ideas.[31]

Look at problems in different ways. This includes thinking about how small children, traditional people, or the elderly would solve the problem. It involves looking at the problem from the perspective of another group.

Make novel combinations. The group can look at the initial list obtained during a brainstorming session which is typical of individuals, and combine them.

Force relationships. Provide the group that formed the initial list with words, pictures, or objects generated from images in magazines or newspapers. The leader can then ask the participants to create connections between the problem and their item. Some sample questions are; "How could this item solve our problem?" What attributes of this item could help us solve our problem?

Make their thoughts visible. Let the individuals doodle and draw, and you never know what ideas may be spurred.

Think in opposites. Ask the opposite group questions. How, for instance, could we ensure no one bought this new product? The responses will illuminate ideas for solving the actual problem.

Think metaphorically. Liken the problem to an item. Pick a random idea/item and ask the group, "How is this item like our problem?"

Prepare. Let the people think about the topic for a while before brainstorming. This will enable them to prepare better.

---

[30] https://www.cleverism.com/18-best-idea-generation-techniques/
[31] http://www.innovationmanagement.se/imtool-articles/eight-ways-to-generate-more-ideas-in-a-group/

Set a Goal. Research shows that giving people a quantity goal before starting the brainstorming session will lead to a long list of ideas to consider. These techniques can also help an individual generate ideas.

6.3 Other Techniques

Other techniques include the scamper method, Brainstorming, mind mapping, synectics, storyboarding, roleplaying, attribute listing, visualization and visual prompts, morphological analysis, forced relationships, daydreaming, reverse thinking, and questioning assumptions, and accidental assumptions genius, brainwriting, wishing, socializing, and collaboration. These methods are presented briefly below (Martin, 2015):

6.3.1 SCAMPER

Scamper is an acronym with each letter standing for an action verb, a prompt for creative ideas. There are nine principal ways you can manipulate a subject. These ways were first formally suggested by Osborn (1953),[32] the father of Brainstorming, and later arranged by Eberle (1972, 1996) into the mnemonic **SCAMPER.**

S = Substitute
C = Combine
A = Adapt
M = Magnify = Modify
P = Put to other uses
E = Eliminate
R = Rearrange = Reverse

You isolate the subject you want to think about and ask the checklist of SCAMPER questions to see what new ideas and thoughts emerge. For example, think about any topic from improving the ordinary paperclip to reorganizing your corporation, and apply the "Scamper" checklist of questions. You'll find that ideas start popping up almost involuntarily as you ask:

Can you substitute something?
Can you combine your subject with something else?
Can you adapt something to your subject?

---

[32] http://www.skymark.com/resources/leaders/osborne.asp

Can you magnify or add to it?
Can you modify or change it in some fashion?
Can you put it to some other use?
Can you eliminate something from it?
Can you rearrange it?
What happens when you reverse it?
- S – Substitute
- C – Combine
- A – Adapt
- M – Modify
- P – Put to another use
- E – Eliminate
- R – Reverse

Martin (2015) presented the following methods:

6.3.2. Brainstorming

The brainstorming process involves engendering a vast number of solutions for a specific problem (idea), emphasizing the number of ideas. Using Brainstorming, there is no assessment of ideas. People voice out their ideas freely even when such ideas are not good. The participants combine ideas to form one good idea, as indicated by the slogan "1+1=3." Brainstorming can be done individually and in groups, typically comprising six to ten people.

Brainstorming is a highly effective problem-solving and idea-generating technique that encourages a group of people to think at the same time creatively about the solution of a specific problem or to come up with an innovative idea. During brainstorming sessions, the participants are encouraged to share all the ideas that come into their heads without being shy or thinking about the quality of the idea. Brainstorming is more about quantity than quality. This technique works best when generating bold, unorthodox ideas that usually would not make the list.

6.3.3. Mind mapping

Mind mapping is a graphical technique for imagining connections between various pieces of information or ideas. Each fact or idea is written down and then connected by curves or lines to its minor or major (previous or following) fact or idea, thus building a web of relationships (Buzan, 1972).

Mapping is utilized in Brainstorming, project planning, problem-solving and note-taking. As with other mapping methods, the intention behind brain mapping is to capture attention and gain and frame information to enable sharing of concepts and ideas. The steps for the participant are writing a key phrase or word in the middle of the page, writing anything else that comes to his mind on the very same page, and then trying to make connections as mentioned in the previous paragraph.

6.3.4. Synectics

Synectics is a creative idea generation and problem-solving technique that arouses thought processes that the subject may not be aware of. It is a rational and creative manner of solving problems introduced by Arthur.[33] Gordon presented three key assumptions that are associated with Synectics research.
- It is possible to describe and teach the creative process
- Invention processes in sciences and the arts are analogous and triggered by the very same "psychic" processes
- Group and individual creativity are analogous

6.3.5. Storyboarding

Storyboarding involves developing a visual story to explain or explore. Storyboards can help creative people represent the information they gained during research. Pictures, quotes from the user and other pertinent information are fixed on a corkboard, or any comparable surface, to stand for a scenario and assist with comprehending the relationships between various ideas.

6.3.6. Roleplaying

In the roleplaying technique, each participant can take on a personality or role different from his own. The technique is fun and can reduce an individual's inhibitions and enable him to come up with unexpected ideas.

---

[33] Gordon (1961), https://www.ideaconnection.com/thinking-methods/synectics-00013html

6.3.7. Attribute listing

Attribute listing is an analytical approach of recognizing new forms of a system or product by identifying/recognizing areas of improvement. One figures out how to enhance a particular product, breaking it into parts. The rest of the steps involve noting the physical features and functions of each component and explaining and studying them to see whether any change or recombination would damage or improve the product.

6.3.8. Visualization and visual prompts

In visualization, the scientist thinks of challenges visually to understand the problem better. Visualization involves incubation and illumination. In the incubation stage, the participant diverts his mind from the problem he is trying to solve and focuses on a different subject. Then, his mind continues to work on the idea subconsciously until it obtains solutions. This stage is called the illumination phase. The method helps brainstorm solutions to innovative challenges involving people and deep psychological or emotional root cause issues.

First, the facilitator distributes a set of pre-selected images – each participant gets one. He also asks the participants to write down whatever ideas come to their minds when they look at the image in their possession. According to Bryan Mattimore,[34] the images should be visually interesting, portraying a diversity of subject matter. In addition, they must depict people in lots of varied kinds of relationships and interactions with other people.

After this, participants pair off and use additional time, sharing and talking about the ideas they have come up with and brainstorming more solutions to the existing problem/challenge. Lastly, the various pairs present their ideas to the rest of the group. Mattimore suggests tailoring the visuals to the nature of the challenge the participants have to solve. However, you should include some irrelevant or random images because these kinds of images may trigger the most innovative solutions.

6.3.9. Morphological analysis

In morphological analysis, the participant recognizes the structural aspects and studies the relationships among them. An example is using a

---

[34] https://thecribb.spaces.nexudus.com/en/blog/read/159299140/18-best-idea-generation-techniques)

powered vehicle to transport an object from one place to another. The important dimensions are the type of vehicle, power source, and medium. For example, the vehicle may be a bed, sling, cart, or chair, while the power source is an electric motor, internal-combustion engine, or pressed air. The object could be conveyed through the air, water or rails. The method can give some novel combinations.

6.3.10. Forced relationships

Inventors can use the method of the forced relationship to join different ideas to obtain a fresh idea. The method results in useful combinations of ideas. Some of the innovations produced include a digital watch that also has a calculator, musical birthday cards, and a Swiss army knife (Robert Olson).

6.3.11 Daydreaming

Daydreaming is not approved by many. However, it can trigger great ideas. It enables a participant to play around with the problem and establish an emotional connection, which helps derive new ideas. Daydreaming focuses on generating ideas irrespective of whether they are practical or not. Many famous inventors used this strategy in the past. An example where this method was employed successfully was the airplane. The Wright brothers allowed their imagination to run wild, thinking about flight.

6.3.12. Reverse thinking

Reverse thinking looks at a challenge in reverse, thinking about opposite ideas. For instance, instead of thinking, 'How do I fill up a gully,' the thought could be 'How do I form a gully and build on it.' Thinking in reverse is much fun. After generating about 10 to 15, one should either continue with a new challenge or else do the reversal once more to make it stronger.

6.3.13. Questioning assumptions

Mattimore suggested how to go about questioning assumptions: The participants should start by settling on the framework for the creative challenge. After this, they should produce 20 to 30 assumptions (irrespective of whether they are true or false). The next step is to select several assumptions from the many generated and utilize them as idea triggers and thought starters to engender fresh ideas.

6.3.14 Accidental genius

Accidental genius is a relatively new technique that utilizes writing to trigger the best ideas, content, and insight.

6.3.15. Brainwriting

Brainwriting is easy. Instead of asking the participants to shout out ideas, the inventor tells them to pen down their thoughts about a specific problem or question for a few minutes. After that, each participant can pass their ideas over to someone else. Next, someone else reads the ideas on the paper and adds some new ones. Allowing another few minutes, the inventor passes each participant's paper to someone else, continuing the process. Finally, after about 15 minutes, you or someone else can collect the sheets from them and post them for instant discussion.

6.3.16 Wishing

This inventor begins the process by asking for the unattainable and then brainstorming ideas to make it a reality or at least an approximation. Also, the team members should collaborate to produce 20 to 30 wishes that pertain to the business. First, the inventor encourages everyone's imagination to run wild with no restrictions on thinking – the more bizarre the idea, the better. The next step is concentrating on a number of these unattainable wishes and utilizing them as creative stimuli to trigger new but more practical ideas. Finally, Mattimore suggested getting the team to challenge the problem from diverse perspectives (imagine how a person from another planet or another industry or profession would view it) or reflect on it. This type of roleplaying assists with moving away from conventional thinking patterns to see fresh possibilities.

6.3.17 Socializing

If employees only hang around with colleagues and friends, they could find themselves in a thinking rut. So let them utilize all those LinkedIn connections to begin some fantastic conversations. Refreshing perspectives will assist with bringing out new thinking and probably, one or two lightning bolts. Socializing in the context of ideation can also be about talking to others about topics that have nothing to do with the present problem.

6.3.18 Collaboration

As the term indicates, collaboration is about two or more people joining hands in working for a common goal. Designers frequently work in groups and engage in collaborative creation in the whole creative process. This approach focuses on three practical techniques that can put you in a creative thinking mode and help you stay there longer.

6.3.19 Using analogies

This technique is very unusual to some people, but it is highly effective. By comparing the similarities between problems, one could generate many ideas. Such analogies will help the inventor realize things about his situations that he missed before and come up with ideas or solutions that otherwise he would have never come up with (Buzan, 1972).

George Hill, *Apostolic Founder and President of Victory Churches International,*[35] said that God has many innovative ideas He wants to share them with us. *"I wisdom dwell with prudence, and find out knowledge of witty inventions"* (Prov. 8:12 KJV). **He presented three things that foster creative Ideas and Witty Inventions.**

1. **Ask God Questions About The Specific Problems Or Opportunities You Face.** This will help prepare your heart for an answer and help you to recognize it as an answer when it comes. Good ideas come from God, so ask Him for one. The world has been marvelously blessed by those who did. *"Call me, and I will answer you and show you great and mighty things that you do not know."* (Jer 33:3)

2. **Expand Your Thinking Power.** God gave us a brain, so let us use it. Let us expand it to recognize and take hold of the *good ideas* available to us. Make time to think about ways of doing things better. Ask yourself, "How can I do it better." **To become a good thinker - do more thinking!** Great thinking comes from good, focused thinking, and once the ideas start flowing, they get better. Make your mind work!

3. **Create an atmosphere where people are not afraid to share their ideas.** Most of the best ideas come together in a team environment.

---

[35] https://victoryusa.org/index.php/about-victory-usa/monthly-leadership teachings/2019/165-February-2019-god-ideas-and-witty-inventions

It is called Creative Collaboration! Creative people encourage and provoke others to think outside of the box (Prov 27:17). As a leader, Hill said, I am glad I do not have to develop all the ideas. However, I need to recognize a good idea when I hear it.

One night, Dr. George Hill said that a friend of John Kilcullen described something he overheard in a bookstore. A customer asked the clerk, "Do you have any simple books on Microsoft DOS? or something like DOS for Dummies?" It was only a passing comment meant to be a joke, but it stuck with Kilcullen, and he did something with it. He launched the "For Dummies" series of books. Some unknown customers had a good idea and did not even know it.

6.4. Thomas Edison's Example

To help us understand the mind of an inventor, we present a summary of the creative habit of Thomas Edison based on the discussion presented in the literature.[36] Thomas Edison had 1,093 patents for inventions that ranged from the lightbulb, the typewriter, electric pen, phonograph, motion picture camera, and alkaline storage battery—to the talking doll and a concrete house that could be built in one day from a cast-iron mold. When he died in 1931, he left 3500 notebooks preserved today in the temperature-controlled vaults of the West Orange Laboratory Archives at the Edison National Historic Site in New Jersey.

The notebooks read like a turbulent brainstorm and present a verbal and visual biography of Edison's mind at work. His notebook, which spanned most of his six-decade career, yielded fresh clues as to how Edison, who had no formal education, could achieve an outstanding inventive record that is still unrivaled. The notebooks illustrate how Edison conceived his ideas from their earliest inceptions and show how he developed and implemented them in great detail. The following are some of Edison's creative-thinking strategies:

1. Go for Quantity

Edison believed that you had to generate many ideas to discover a good idea. He expected one minor invention every ten days and a major creation every six months. It took over 50,000 experiments to invent the alkaline storage cell battery and 9000 to perfect the light bulb. Edison looked at creativity as simply good, honest, hard work. He believed that

---

[36] https://thinkjarcollective.com/tools/thomas-edisons-creative-thinking-habits/

invention is 99% perspiration and 1% inspiration. Increasing one's idea production requires conscious effort.

A specific quota focuses one's energy in a competitive way that guarantees fluency and flexibility of thought. Initial ideas are usually poorer in quality than later ideas. Just as water must run from a faucet for a while to be clean, so thought must flow before it becomes creative. Therefore, the first ideas are usually natural thoughts.

A way to guarantee the productivity of creative thought is to give oneself an idea quota. For instance, assign an idea quota of 40 ideas if you are looking for ideas alone or a quota of 120 ideas if a group is brainstorming for ideas. The first third will be the same-old ideas. The second third will be more interesting, and the last third will show more insight, curiosity, and complexity.

2. Challenge Assumptions

Edison felt his lack of formal education was, in fact, "his blessing." This enabled him to approach his invention work with far fewer assumptions than his more educated competitors. Moreover, his wild enthusiasm inspired him to challenge assumptions consistently.

He felt that, in some ways, too much education corrupted people by prompting them to make so many assumptions that they were unable to see many of nature's great possibilities. So, he hired assistants who were willing to try out things first without making assumptions.

3. Nothing is Wasted

Edison would always ask what the failure revealed when an experiment failed and would enthusiastically record what he had learned. His notebooks contain pages of material on what he learned from his abortive ideas, including his many experiments on willpower (he conducted countless experiments with rubber tubes extended from his forehead, trying to will the physical movement of a pendulum).

Edison relentlessly recorded and illustrated every problem worked on in his notebooks. In addition, Edison would review his notebooks to rethink ideas and inventions he had abandoned in the past in light of what he'd recently learned whenever he succeeded with a new idea. If he were mentally blocked from working on a new idea, he would review his notebooks to see if there was some thought or insight that could trigger a new approach.

Edison would often jot down his observations of the natural world, failed patents, research papers written by other inventors, and ideas others had come up with in other fields. He would also routinely comb various publications for novel ideas that sparked his interest and record them in his notebooks. He advised his assistants to make it a habit to keep on the lookout for novel and exciting ideas that others have used successfully on other problems in other fields. One's idea needs to be original only in its adaptation to the problem one is working on.

Edison's practice was to record his ideas and other novel ideas in a notebook— call it. Then, when confronted with a problem, he reviewed his notebook and looked for ways to cross-fertilize ideas, techniques, and conceptual models by transferring them from one problem to the next.

4. **Constantly Improve Your Ideas and Products and Those of Others**

Contrary to popular belief, Edison did not invent the light bulb: instead, he perfected the bulb as a consumer item. Edison also studied all his inventions and ideas as springboards for other designs and ideas in their own right. The telephone (sounds transmitted) suggested the phonograph (sounds recorded), which suggested motion pictures (images recorded). He believed that every new idea is some addition or modification to something that already exists. Therefore, one can take a subject and manipulate or change it into something else using SCAMPER as presented earlier.

Edison persisted in using the trial-and-error method until he obtained a workable idea. There was a staggering display of hundreds of phonograph horns of every shape, size, and material in Edison's laboratory. Edison built many visual objects, used some, and rejected others. He tried out every possible design he could conceive of. He never quit working on his subject until he had tried many ideas. We should cultivate the following creative-thinking habits:

- **When looking for ideas, create lots of ideas.**
- **Consistently challenge assumptions.**
- **Record your ideas and the ideas of others in a notebook.**
- **Learn from your failures and the failures of others.**
- **Constantly look for ways to improve your ideas and products and the ideas and products of others.**

6.5 Areas We Need God to Open Our Eyes

6.5.1 Security

Innovation ensures security. God has promised His children all-around protection, so we should not live in fear. He said He would bless our going out, and our coming in (Deut.28). A thousand shall fall by our right and ten thousand by our left, and nothing shall harm us. He said that we shall behold the end of the wicked (Ps. 91). He keeps watch over us while we sleep, and He neither sleeps nor slumbers. He is not human to feel tired or overwhelmed by the multitude of armed robbers or the sophistication of weapons. Trust in Him is far better than trusting in modern security outfits that can still disappoint or fail.

However, God still expects us to use any possible human means to protect ourselves when necessary while we still have absolute faith in Him as our protector.

6.5.2 Amory

King Uzziah was a very prosperous king of Judah. During his reign, he made machines invented by skillful men. His men stationed the machines at towers to shoot arrows and haul great stones at his enemies (II Chr. 26:15). These innovations brought protection to his subjects and secured his kingdom against the intrusion of the armies of the neighboring countries; they brought him fame and prosperity.

Again, like in the case of his great grandfather, King Solomon, as men paid visits to admire the wonder of his military strength, they brought gifts that enriched him the more. Innovations can generate wealth.

God can open your eyes to innovate military wares that will result in prosperity. First, however, note that peaceful crisis resolution is far better than going to war. The former conserves resources and preserves lives and property. The latter is retrogressive. However, when it comes to war, where all efforts to sue for peace fail, like David, we can say, "He teaches my hands to war, so that my arms can bend a bow of bronze" (Ps. 18:34; 144:1; 2Sam. 22:35).

6.5.3 Military Intelligence

God is a master strategist in all areas of life, be it in the military, business, education, sports, etc. As the creator, He embodies wisdom, knowledge, and understanding. I am always excited when I read the Bible and notice that God's knowledge revealed in the scriptures through His Holy prophets several thousand years ago is relevant today. God revealed some of these even before man started thinking about them. For instance, while men were still arguing and trying to prove that the earth is flat, God had already stated that it is round. The recent general acceptance of the earth's roundness resulted in reworking the earth theories to conform to the new knowledge. The scriptures provide adequate basic knowledge for people in all areas of life.

Militarily, God is also a master strategist. He exhibited military intelligence several times when the Israelites had to fight against their enemies. No wonder He instructed Joshua to meditate on the scriptures so that he would do well as an army field general. Meditating on the word and obeying the scriptures was what he handed out as a prerequisite for success. Not only did meditation and obedience equip him with natural intelligence, but they were to link him with the inexhaustible source of power and wisdom and faith which could move mountains.

He had to command in one of the epic battles, "Sun stand still, the moon...." and God honored the faith-motivated words. After man had done the scientific analysis and discovered that the total sum of the days did not add up and that the difference is traceable to the gap created by two miracles that set the times back, it is surprising some still argue that the scriptures are not true.

This book of the law shall not depart from your mouth, but you should meditate on it day and night, and by so doing, you will make your way prosperous (Joshua 1:8). Blessed is the man that walks not in the counsel of the wicked; nor stands in the way of sinners; nor sits in the seats of the scornful. But his delight is in the word of the Lord. In the word of the Lord does he meditate day and night; he shall be like a seed planted by the river. Its leaves shall not wither, but it shall bring forth fruits in its own season, and whatever he does shall prosper (Ps. 1:1-3).

The military strategies applied by God are many. It seems that by using all these strategies, He wanted to show His infinite supremacy and many colors of His wisdom in dealing with issues. He could have as well applied one technique in all cases. His approach teaches us that we should not be stereotyped; instead, we should appraise each problem carefully and the correct strategy applied. While experience is necessary and relying on it is valuable, it may never take the place of relying on God, whose infinite knowledge is unquestionably accurate.

The following are some of the techniques he exhibited:

i) Military Intelligence – reveals place, time
ii) Ambushed
iii) Using elements – hail, earthquake, landslides, rain, snow, etc.
iv) Surprise attack
v) Confusion
vi) Siege

6.6 Technology

The flying scroll is another example of how God can use the scriptures to reveal to man an idea that could revolutionize the world. Someone had a revelation of the flying scroll in the Book of Isaiah as a modern way of communicating Christian messages across the globe to build up the body of Christ. Since then, the ministry has grown in gigantic measures to bring great blessings to people. A Christian shouldn't grope about for ideas and knowledge when he has God as his creator, the Lord Jesus as His wisdom, and the Holy Ghost as the revealer of all truth and teacher. God made us in His image. Since God is creative and innovative, we should share in this aspect of His characteristics. Like father like son, they say.

6.7 Business

God can also reveal to someone hidden things about business or some business secrets he would apply and prosper. A certain pauper was jobless. Instead of whiling away his time in idleness, he struck a business deal with a trader who sells footwear in a particular shop in a market. He would purchase a few pairs on credit, take them to another market part, and sell them. After selling the goods, he would pay his debts and continued that way and gradually built enough capital to establish his shop and become a distributor. Jobless youths have much to learn from this man.

CHAPTER SEVEN

ENHANCING OUR ABILITY TO RECEIVE REVELATION

7.1 Introduction

Certain qualities enhance our ability to receive revelation. God may decide to speak anytime, anywhere, and under any circumstance, yet some factors facilitate our receiving revelation.

7.2 Beam Versus Specks

Isa. 6:1-4 – Isaiah was crying woes unto others because he was blind about his own deprivations. He couldn't see where he was failing. His deficiencies were hidden from him. Many today can only see faults in what others say or do but never in their own lives. In their own judgment, they are better than others, and they are never at fault. We need to come to the point where we see others as better than ourselves (Phil. 2:3), where we judge ourselves rightly and see our deprivations as we are. Then, like Isaiah, we will examine our lives first and remove the big log of wood blinding us before we attempt removing the specks in another person's eyes. It is doubtful if one could have many revelations when his mind is blind to his faults. Notice that Isaiah's revelation of his self-deprivations came before great revelation.

7.3 Singleness of Purpose

The Bible says, "The light of the body is the eye: if your eye is single, your whole body shall be full of light. But if your eye is evil, thy whole body shall be full of darkness. If, therefore, the light in thee be darkness, how great [is] that darkness!" (Mt. 6: 22-23).

Singleness of the eye represents singleness of purpose. A divided mind is hard to deal with. A person so afflicted is unstable in all of his ways. Indecision is frustrating, and it prevents decisive action. But a person who does not know whether he will serve the Lord or not, and puts off accepting salvation through Jesus Christ, is deciding default! Those who can only see what the flesh and the devil desire will make decisions in the dark! Spiritual truths will not influence their decisions, nor will they be made in the light of eternal interests. Singleness of purpose is essential in receiving revelation.

7.4 Viewing Position

Naturally, the extent we can see with our eyes depends on our viewing position. For instance, when someone is flying at an elevation of hundreds of kilometers, the gigantic buildings, which used to tower several meters above a man standing on the earth, become very minute from an airplane. The higher the location of the airplane, the smaller the building. In fact, at some heights above, it dwindles into the size of a pinhead. This evident phenomenon also has a spiritual connotation. The viewing position affects the amount of revelation a Christian receives. The more we realize our exalted position in Christ, the more materialism with all its enticement and allurement pale into insignificance. The more we can see the earth from God's perspective, the more detached we are from wealth.

Earthly things influence some of us because we are always in the valley. The Israelites never had a mountain experience. The further they went was to mill around the foot of the mountain while Moses and Joshua were on the mountain interacting with God. Was there any wonder that unbelief and things of this world distracted them as soon as Moses was away! They became engrossed with food, drink, and merriment,

God raised us together with Christ and sat us in the heavenly places in him, at the right hand of God, a place of authority, righteousness, and joy. Observing the earth from that vantage position where the principalities and powers are made subject to Christ, it is evident that our perspective of the earth and the universe will be very different from that of a person on the earth. From that vantage position, the earth dwindles into insignificance.

When God wanted to change man's perspective, He had always invited him to the mountain. It was either a place where ultimate sacrifice was paid or a place of issuing the law. Abraham sacrificed Isaac at Mount Moriah. Jesus had to die at Mount Calvary. God instructed Moses to go up the mount, where he showed him the largeness and beauty of the promised land before he died. Moses received the law at Mount Sinai. When the devil wanted to tempt Jesus, he took Him to the highest point in the temple where he could observe as much of the earth as possible. The devil wanted to change the perception Jesus had of the world and his devilish kingdom. He thought that by showing the Lord the wealth and glory of this earth from that exhilarating sight, he would entice Him to sell out.

Jesus took His three disciples to the mountain of transfiguration. He wanted to show the three inner disciples His glory and the sole authority He had like the perfect, sinless son of God and end the contention about who had the kingdom. He wanted to show that it was not Moses, though he was the most outstanding leader who discussed with God face to face, the receiver of the law; neither was it Elijah, the great representative of all the prophets, who went to heaven without death. So, we should listen to Jesus in this age.

Apart from the apparent fact that mountains possess other physical characteristics such as serenity and cool temperature, which make them conducive to more intimate interaction with God, they offer the advantage of seclusion from the hustles and bustles of life. In addition, they are suitable for sightseeing. Many have done exhilarating sports out of mountain climbing.

We need to pray that God will lead us to the mountain top, from where we can have a better perspective of ourselves, of our Lord, and the earthly things. It will change our value system. We will set our priority and want to make our permanent abode at the mountain top with the Lord Jesus like the apostle Peter or at least visit it regularly.

The problem with the church is that so many Christians are wasting in the valley. The Scripture says none wants to take hold of God. Many are satisfied with the below Christian-like experience; none wants to live an everyday Christian life. The normal Christian life is a life of holiness, faith, and miracles. The church can only attend that life when it begins to live at the mountain tops.

7.5 Clarity of Vision

"Moreover, the Word of the Lord came unto me, saying, Jeremiah, what sees thou?" And I said, I see a rod of an almond tree. Then said the Lord unto me, Thou hast seen well: for I will hasten my word to perform it.

God gave Jeremiah a series of messages by speaking to him directly and through visions. The above passage was just the first of the visions about God's Word and His eagerness to fulfill it.

He wanted to be sure Jeremiah saw the right vision – a rod of an almond tree. What one sees is very important. Why? What we see informs the type of perception we have about that subject or thing. Did we see it completely or partially? Sometimes what view or picture we hold in our mind about a person affects our attitude towards that thing or person.

Numerous visions from God have been misinterpreted because we did not see them well. We have only seen a part of them. Why do photographers take a shot from different positions and views? They help us have a complete view of that object. Often a single view may not be enough. For example, a man wants to marry a wife and is interested in a girl who lives abroad, a girl he has not met before, and, if he wants to know her shape, he doesn't just need to see the front elevation. While the back or front view will reveal how broad the hip is, the side elevation will show the extent of protrusion. What we see affects if we accept or reject the person. I have heard people say, "I didn't know he was like that. I thought he was different." Those misconceptions were nursed by the initial perception of the person's character. As they have more contact, that perception may change for good or bad.

CHAPTER EIGHT

POSITIVE ATTITUDES TOWARD SUCCESS

8.1 Lift up Your Eyes

The field is ripe. Jesus told the disciples to lift their eyes and see that the harvest was ripe. How could Jesus have said that when the Pharisees were all over the place opposing His mission and trying to stifle the life out of Him? How could He have said that amid vehement rejection of His mission and person? It takes God opening the eyes of a Christian to see that the field is ripe and the souls of men are ready for harvest. Amid all the negative reactions He was receiving, He saw beyond the physical to perceive the readiness of men and women to receive the message. His mission was not strangulated by the opposition. He never allowed himself to be discouraged by those who needn't receive Him. "He went to His own, and they rejected Him." He didn't rest until He had achieved what He set out to do.

Similarly, we should look beyond the physical and tap from the supernatural to see that the harvest is already ripe. God made each man for a purpose which He expects Him to fulfill. He knew all the discouraging situations, the problems, and apathy all around. In the midst of all that, we should observe the opportunities that abound. The economic condition in Nigeria and corrupt practices are reasonable grounds to brood the seed of innovation. Instead of looking at the unripe fields, we should rather be positive and focus on the advantages created by our situation, receive and implement innovative ideas.

Another example of a positive attitude was the case of Paul when the soldiers took him to Rome with the other prisoners. The prisoners, Roman soldiers, sailors, and other passengers totaled 276. En route to Rome, their ship sailed under turbulent storms and opposing currents. Subsequently, the ship sank. Paul refused to be downcast under the terrible conditions during which the crew and passengers were downcast, frustrated, and lived in suspense and loss of appetite. He prayed for them. Encouraged by the revelation he received from God, he remained positive and became a source of blessing and encouragement to all. It all depends on how we look at our predicament, either complaining and grumbling all day long or singing praises in the night of pain, imprisonment and loneliness. But in all, the choice is ours. Spending time on the negative aspect, dwelling on all the evil that has befallen us and our country, is fruitless. It makes us sadder and instills in us hopelessness, fear, disgruntlement, and desire to flee the country. It saps us of the little energy we have to invest in positive, creative thinking and productivity.

8.2 Looking for A city

We look not at the physical things but at those things that are spiritual, for the material things are temporary, but the spiritual ones are eternal. It is a matter of focus on the physical or spiritual. The physical things are splendid, alluring, and captivating. They are the things our five senses can easily perceive. We can spend all our lives in the pursuit of grabbing and making them our own. But they are ephemeral.

Unfortunately, people can kill and maim others to have them. People are often deluded into believing that these things have eternal values, but they are not. The Scripture says that man is like the flower in the field that radiates warmth and beauty in the morning, but in the afternoon, it withers away. But he that does the will of God abides forever.

The Patriarchs of old were looking for a city whose builder was God. They focused on the eternal things, not on the temporary ones, which have no eternal values. While we try to innovate and create things after God, our maker, we must understand and appreciate that whatever we make is temporary and transient. One day, they will become old, and new ideas will spring up, resulting in better products. Only what God created can be perfect and will require no improvement.

8.3 The Nature of Revelation

8.3.1 God's Ways Are Unpredictable

God is God the creator, omniscient and Omnipotent. He can decide to use anything or anyone under seemingly unrealistic circumstances to achieve His purpose. So, you should be ever prepared to look out for the unique opportunities He creates. God often uses unlikely persons and circumstances. We tend to look outward instead of relying on the whispers from a renewed mind, which are usually more accurate because they are from God. Jesus was born in an unlikely place under unlikely circumstances. There was nothing special about His parenthood, yet, His coming into the world brought inestimable blessings and salvation to man.

8.3.2 Little Fishes

God may want us to start small. He often uses small things and causes them to grow big. The kingdom of God started small, like a mustard seed, and has now grown very big. That tiny seed of an idea can develop further as you brood over it and consider it prayerfully from every angle. As you break it into parts, it could multiply like the two fishes and five loaves of bread.

8.3.3 God Wants to Open Your Eyes

God is in the business of opening people's eyes to see the opportunities around them or to realize such opportunities. He wants blind people to regain their sight. He asked the blind man, "Do you want to receive your sight?" I am throwing back at you that same question. Tell the Lord that you want to see. If you are not seeing, it is either because you are content with staying blind or ignorant. Either state is a very limiting one. "My people perish for lack of knowledge." Paul prayed for the Ephesian Christians that God would open the eyes of their understanding to know the enormous love God has for them, and the greatness of the power that works in them.

God has given us everything we need in this world to excel. If the unbelievers can have ideas and develop them, we can even do far better because of our relationship with God. Consider the following facts:

i) We are His sons
ii) Heirs and joint-heirs with Jesus
iii) We have the Holy Ghost

iv) We are God's children

The unbelievers can operate as God's children only. They knew Him at the creator level, and the much they can receive from Him is like the crumbs that fell off the table. But pause a little and ponder all the great inventions and innovations men have created simply because they are descendants of Adam. God allows His rain to fall both on the wicked and the righteous because He is a great and generous God.

Unbelievers can also receive inspiration because God has imbued every man and woman with one form of talent or the other. As they discover their abilities and then move on to develop them, they achieve greatness through diligence and hard work. But that is the only level at which an unbeliever can operate. He could only tap from his natural inspiration, which is still very powerful. But as God's sons, we have far much more.

Sonship

As sons, we are heirs of what He has and joint-heirs with the Lord. To imagine how big our inheritance is, consider the greatness and vastness of God's creation. In addition, as people who have a special relationship with Him, we can pray and receive our requests. Consider I Cor. 2: 8 – 12

None of the rulers of this age or world perceived and recognized and understood this, for they would never have crucified the Lord of Glory if they had. But on the contrary, as the Scripture says, "What eye has not seen and ear has not heard. It has not entered into the heart of man, (all that) God has prepared (made and keeps ready) for those who love Him (who hold Him in affectionate reverence promptly obeying Him and gratefully recognizing the benefits He has bestowed)" (see also Isa 64:4; 65:17).

Yet to us God has unveiled and revealed them by and through His Spirit for the (Holy) Spirit searches diligently, exploring and examining everything, even sounding the profound and bottomless things of God (the divine counsels and things hidden and beyond man's scrutiny).

Now we have not received the spirit (that belongs to) the world, but the (Holy) spirit who is from God, (given to us) that we might realize and comprehend and appreciate the gifts (of divine favor and blessing so freely and lavishly) bestowed on us by God.

What a marvelous truth that the natural, non-spiritual man does not understand and accept. First, we notice that the devil did not know all the truths when he set out to orchestrate the death of Jesus. If he had known

God's purpose, he would not have crucified the Lord. The death and resurrection of the Lord brought us salvation from the ravages of sin, the guilt of sin, freedom from sicknesses and diseases, and enduring peace and joy in the Holy Ghost. In addition, His death drew us close to God and we became a chosen generation, a royal priesthood, a peculiar people treasured by God. That was not all. We became the righteousness of God created in Christ Jesus. Jesus became our wisdom and righteousness (I Cor. 1:30).

Jesus was the embodiment of all wisdom and knowledge. His eternal spirit is in us, and we have the mind of Christ, which knows and understands the counsels and purposes of God (I Cor. 2:16).

Second, God has prepared certain precious things for those who love Him. What are those things? Are those things only the things in heaven to be enjoyed when we get there? I do not think so. These should include special revelations that He will show us if we ask Him. They are the great and mighty things, plans, purposes, knowledge, and revelations. So, if you really love God, ask Him to open your eyes. Just a drop of such an idea or revelation in any discipline or works of life will change you, your family, and your society and bring glory to His name. Jesus said, "All things are ours."

The natural man can never access these hidden things. They are revealed to us through the Holy Spirit. Notice how unlimited the extent of revelation we can receive from God. The issue is that we have the Spirit of God, which knows the creator's mind. He was there when the world was created. He allows us to access the great and mighty things we do not know. We can easily explain this in another way using King Saul's experience before he became the king.[37] His donkeys had just gotten missing, and he searched for them all over the place. Then, he met Samuel, who God used to reveal their location to him through the Word of knowledge. That is what the Holy Spirit can do. He can tell the truth to us. He can enable us to see into the future and guide us to make decisions that will favor us.

All things are Ours

God has given us everything we need to excel. For His divine power has bestowed upon us all things that (are requisite and suited) to life and godliness, through the (full, personal knowledge of Him who called us by and to His glory and excellence (virtue) (II Pet. 1:3).

---

[37] 1 Sam 9

You can

Whatever idea He reveals to you, rest assured that He will guide you into achieving great success. God wants to give us the best. The only problem is if we can believe and trust Him to do what He has planned for us. We can do all things through Christ who strengthens us. He will teach you how to develop the idea and succeed. God said, "...I am the Lord your God, who teaches you to profit, who leads you in the way you should go" (Isa. 48:17). You are not alone. God will guide you all the way.

8.4 Deceitfulness

Deceitfulness is the art of presenting oneself or one's actions in a wrong way. The person's intention is usually to register a false impression of himself before the other person to gain an advantage. Many so-called friends have been revealed to be deceitful, which was only after the harm was already done. A popular example from one of the Shakespearian novels was where Ceaser trusted his friend, Brutus, so considerably; yet he was the very one that killed him.

Judas betrayed Jesus with a kiss. Joab, David's General Army Commander, was able to kill Abner, King Saul's Commander, with a kiss. Each evil man used the kiss and action to depict love, first to deceive, confuse and win the victim's confidence. And when the victim was taken in, the real action, murder was perpetrated. What bothers me is not whether deceitful friends exist. It is not even if some of my friends are deceitful, which I can attest to, but how to always be on alert to perceive their strategies and avoid the traps they are setting against me. But much more dangerous is even the tendency of two other 'friends' I have. From the onset, I know one of them to be evil while the other to be good, and they always tend to be around me to entice me. I am talking about sin and riches. The Scripture says, "But warn (admonish, urge, and encourage) one another every day, as long as it is called Today, that none of you may be hardened (into settled rebellion) by the deceitfulness of sin (by the fraudulence, the stratagem, the trickery which the delusive glamour of his sin may play on him" Heb. 3:13).

"And the ones sown among the thorns are others who hear the Word. Then the cares and anxieties of the world and distractions of the age and the pleasure and delight and false glamour and deceitfulness of riches ... creep in and choke and suffocate the Word, and it becomes fruitless." (Mk. 4:18 – 19).

We need God to open our eyes to see the wonderful opportunities around us to create wealth and fulfill our responsibilities and destinies and to perceive when the very blessings we have become instruments in the hands of the devil. We need God to open our eyes to understand the relationship between riches and sin and the fraudulence, stratagem, and trickery that sin's delusive glamour can play on us. Because of how crucial this is and the danger inherent in the sin, we should admonish one another about the dangers of sin, urge one another to desist from sin; and encourage ourselves to live holy lives.

8.4.1 Deception of Riches

Wealth deceives people in the following ways:

i) Lasts for eternity

A person possessing wealth may be deceived to believe that his wealth will last till eternity. He may find it difficult to accept that wealth and riches are ephemeral. His wrong notion affects how he handles it, either being stingy or liberal in giving to worthy causes. It takes God to open one's eyes to understand how wealth can be used as one's slave instead of as a master. No matter how wealthy a man is he will leave all the wealth one day. "...for we came to the earth with nothing, and we shall certainly leave with nothing."

ii) Buys everything

Many tend to believe that money and wealth can buy everything. While the importance of wealth and money is great, there are several things people may still pass through in life, specific ugly experiences where money cannot be of value. For example, when one is sick with certain ailments, he can receive attention in the world's best hospitals and be healed. But there are other cases millions are spent in hospitals, yet the sick person dies.

Money also cannot buy true love. Some ladies may be interested in a man because of his wealth, while others cannot have any relationship with a man simply because of his wealth. If they do not love the man, they will not even accept his gifts not to talk of his advances, or go into a contractual marriage agreement with him.

iii) Greater than Live

There is also the tendency to accept that wealth is more important than life. Hence, some accumulate wealth without spending it to save lives. Instead, jeopardize their lives, almost to death, to have it.

CHAPTER NINE

MEDITATION

9.1 Introduction

The Hebrew word for meditating is 'hagah' which means to murmur (in pleasure or anger), ponder, imagine, meditate, mourn, mutter, roar, speak, study, talk, and utter. This Word we usually interpret to mean only mutter stands for many other things. But how relevant are the other meanings in the various verses where the word 'meditate' was used? I would think that all the meanings are relevant as they reveal additional important ways to meditate appropriately and hence receive the precious blessings accruing from meditation.

We must bear in mind as we go on that the whole essence of meditation is to know and to obey. In order words, through meditation, the mind is renewed by the cleansing and transforming power of the Word. In that transformed stage, it becomes easier to know God's good, acceptable and perfect will and put it into practice (Rom. 12: 1-2). All the experiences represented by each of the above action words can manifest as one truly meditates on the Word of God. They may not all manifest at the same sitting as one meditates, but they are actions involved when one's mind dwells on the Word. God expects Joshua to meditate on the Word through pondering, studying, speaking, and so on that, it transforms him to know the right thing to do each moment.

Before we comment further, notice what Colossians 2:16 (AMPC) says: "Let the word (spoken by) Christ (the Messiah) have its home (in your hearts and minds) and dwell in you in (all its) richness, as you teach and admonish and train one another in all insight and intelligence and wisdom (in spiritual things, and as you sing) psalms and hymns and spiritual songs, making melody to God with (His) grace in your hearts."

There are times when I have gotten deep revelation meditating on the Word of God that my heart was immersed in deep, unexplainable liquid joy. Under that situation, I find myself murmuring in pleasure or shouting (roaring) in wonder. I could only concur with David that the Word is sweeter than honey. At other times, I have studied the Word and meditated on it that I felt only ashamed of myself and repented with tears in my eyes. That is the two-edged sword for you – causing joy on one hand and causing compunction and sadness on the other. The Word of God is profitable for instruction, reproof, the conviction of sin, and correction of error and discipline (II Tim 3:16). Have you meditated on the Word to the point that it convicted you, and you started shedding tears? That is one way the Word transforms us.

Another word is "to ponder." Pondering over the Word is an act of deep thinking. According to the Oxford English Dictionary, it means to think about something carefully for a period of time. It is synonymous with consider. We should create time to ponder what we have read or studied in the Bible. That is the only way to remember it and make it part of us. Any person who reads the Bible without pondering is like the seed that fell on the wayside in the parable of the Sower. The Word couldn't take root in the hearts of the hearers. It was so exposed that the birds of the air saw it and devoured it. If the Word is thought over and its implications for our lives are carefully realized, then it will bear fruits. There is no way the enemy will steal it. We need to lodge the Word deep in our hearts through repetition and careful thinking where the devil cannot easily steal it until it germinates and bears fruits.

We often do not take the issue of meditation seriously. We listen to sermons and get excited while in the church. But as soon as we leave the premises, we have forgotten what we learned. We have no time to consider or ponder over what we learned. No plan to go through the points put down— no time to reflect on its applications in our lives. We come back the following Sunday the same as we were several weeks ago. The words we hear do not impact us because we do not create time to ponder over what we have listened to like the noble Berean Christians (Acts 17:11).

The next point is to imagine what we have studied. Imagining the Word of God and talking about it is a way of boosting our faith. When we confess the positive things we have learned, our faith soars. It helps to remove doubts, and as we think and confess it, it happens because as a man thinks in his heart, so he is.

Studying the Word of God also widens our capacity to meditate and receive revelations. We meditate on what we have studied to make the results part of us. When the words find a home in us, with good nourishment and constant muttering and talking, the seed of the Word germinates, grows, and bears fruit. Whether we speak or talk as the outcome of meditation or during meditation depends on how excited we are about our new insight. We can become so excited that we want to talk to a friend in an informal setting or make a sermon out of it in a formal setting. Whichever, it should be noted that God has fashioned all these steps to enable us to remember and become more acquainted with the Word as we repeat it.

Christian meditation is a form of prayer in which a structured attempt is made to become aware of and reflect upon the revelations of God. The Word meditation comes from the Latin Word meditārī, which has a range of meanings, including reflecting on, studying, and practicing meditation. By sitting or lying comfortably, closing one's eyes, and pondering about God's Word, one will receive the blessings associated with meditation. We must think deeply and reflect on our beliefs and actions. Without this introspection, we can forget the importance of living righteously and following the lessons of the Bible. Colossians 3: 16 stated: "Let the word (spoken by) Christ (the Messiah) have its home (in your hearts and minds) and dwell in you in (all its) richness as you teach and admonish and train one another in all insight and intelligence and wisdom [in spiritual things, and as you sing] Psalms and hymns and spiritual songs making melody to God with (His) grace in our hearts."

God expects us to use all methods – muttering, singing, talking to ourselves, writing, and so on – to make sure the Word doesn't depart from us. Notice that the Word should dwell in our hearts and mind. That is, it should have its home or abode in us. We should be an embodiment of the Word of God through study and meditation, repetition, and confession. It should settle in our minds, renewing them and enlightening our thoughts; dwell in our hearts, and control our affections. God has programmed it to transform our lives. To what extent should the Word dwell in us? It should dwell in us richly and not sparsely. We should know the Word of God such that it practically oozes out from us. The Word is the seed for success, and we should sow it plentiful in our hearts; otherwise, we shall not know and appropriate all the wonderful blessings God has for us.

With the word dwelling in us richly, we can teach, admonish, and train. We need to meditate on these things even to succeed in teaching, admonishing, or training others successfully, without simply dishing out the letters only, that kill. We should do these in all insight, intelligence, and wisdom. God created intelligence and wisdom, which He has always displayed in all his works and dealings with man. We should fill our minds with wisdom and intelligence as we teach, admonish and train others so that we can have the grace to edify and not tear down. Sometimes, without asking for the help of the Holy Ghost, we dabble in admonishing others carelessly. The result is making the person move further away from God.

Some of us consider 'Intelligence' to be carnal, so we do not appreciate its relationship with our Christian work. God is intelligent as well as wise. The logic and sequence He exhibited in creation show His high level of intelligence. One cannot fully comprehend His wisdom. We are not to teach, admonish and train others casually but carefully and diligently. Whether we are teaching, singing, or preaching, God wants us to prepare well so that He can approve us. Sometimes, we get up late Sunday morning and rush to the church to lead in praise and worship or preach the sermon without adequately renewing our minds and spending time with God. Under such a condition, we shouldn't expect a miracle unless God, out of His providence as He does sometimes, decides to work wonders despite us. But He expects us to use the intelligence He has given us to prepare as much as possible, trusting Him that He will use us as we are.

The benefits of meditation are as follows:

9.2 Brings us closer to God

One of the debilitating cultures of our times is the lack of meditation. Preoccupation with social media and having itching eyes for any news have grossly reduced our time for meditation. This spiritual exercise was one of the crucial instructions God instructed Joshua to indulge in if he were to be a successful leader. Unfortunately, this has been replaced by involvement in reading all manner of news that fills our minds with sadness and hopelessness and leaves us bankrupt.

Meditating on the personality of God and His works has a way of not only bringing us closer to God and hence transforming us into His nature but also equipping us with His creative mind to think and act like Him. "I remember the days of long ago; I meditate on all your works and consider what your hands have done" (Psalm 143:5).

9.3 Transforms

Meditating on the Scriptures is the key to personal transformation, becoming increasingly like Jesus, developing higher faith in our Lord, and thinking creatively like God. God wants us to be like Him, be innovative and creative like Him, and be resourceful like Him - like father, like son. (See also Chapter 11).

9.4 Removes Anxiety and Solves Health Problems

Meditation removes anxiety and stress as a man focuses his mind on the Word of God. In addition, meditation can also reduce:

i) Insomnia
ii) Depression
iii) Post-traumatic syndrome disorder (PTSD)
iv) Attention deficit hyperactivity disorder (ADHD)
v) Autism
vi) Addictions

As he meditates on God's Word and appropriates in his heart the promises, the mind becomes quiet, and free from anxiety and is filled with joy and peace and reduces stress. That he is free from anxiety increases the chances of getting one's prayers answered, boosts faith, increases his confidence in the Word, and draws him closer to God. God "will keep in perfect peace those whose minds are steadfast, because they trust in you" (Isaiah 26:3). "My son, pay attention to what I say; turn your ear to my words. Do not let them out of your sight, keep them within your heart; for they are life to those who find them and health to one's whole body" (Proverbs 4:20-22).

Research has shown that some stressed-induced sicknesses are healed when we eliminate anxiety and worry. The Word of God is full of God's promises which can help us enjoy the peace of mind needed for our well-being. The Lord said, "The peace I give to you, not as the world gives .... Be of good cheer. I have overcome the world" (John 16: 33). "Be anxious about nothing but in everything through prayers and supplications with thanksgiving let your request be made known unto God and the peace of God which passes all understanding shall keep your hearts and mind in Christ Jesus" (Phil. 4: 6, 7).

9.4.1 Helps us Gain Control Over Our thoughts

The practice of meditation is such a valuable tool for gaining control over our thoughts, correcting focus, and setting intentions. As a result, one gets calmer and learns to take life in one's stride and don't get irritated by minor annoyances.

One's thinking tends to get creative.

9.5 Key to Success

God told Joshua, "This Book of the law shall not depart out of your mouth, but you shall meditate on it day and night, that you may observe and do according to all that is written in it. For then you shall make your way prosperous, and then you shall deal wisely and have success." The word "depart" in Hebrew means to withdraw, cease, depart, go back, remove, takeaway (Strongs, 1988).

Joshua obeyed God and meditated on the word day and night. As a result, he developed enough faith to believe that God would honor his command to extend the day until he vanquished his enemies. Likewise, when we meditate on the Word of God, accept it, and confess it, we have our miracle. As God opens our eyes to understand and appropriate one promise or the other, we should remember the role of meditation, believing in it, and confession play to ensure success.

In Psalm 1, the Scripture states, "Blessed is the one who does not walk in step with the wicked or stand in the way that sinners take or sit in the company of mockers, but whose delight is in the law of the LORD, and who meditates on his law day and night.

He is like a tree planted by streams of water, which yields its fruit in season and whose leaf does not wither— whatever he does prosper. Not so the wicked! They are like chaff that the wind blows away. Therefore, the wicked will not stand in the judgment, or sinners in the assembly of the righteous. For the LORD watches over the way of the righteous, but the way of the wicked leads to destruction."

The mouth is used to mutter, mumble, talk, speak, shout advice, sing, worship, greet, etc. The Word of God should not cease from our lips. We should keep on saying it. Sometimes, we emphasize the meditation aspect and leave the saying aspect which is equally important.

9.6 It Builds Faith

No wonder King David was a man full of faith. He meditated on the Word as he lay on his bed and all the day long, as evidenced by the following passages:

Psalm 4:4: Tremble and do not sin; search your hearts and be silent when you are on your beds.

Psalm 19:14: May these words of my mouth and this meditation of my heart be pleasing in your sight, LORD, my Rock, and my Redeemer.

Psalm 49:3: My mouth will speak words of wisdom; the meditation of my heart will give you understanding.

Psalm 63:6: On my bed, I remember you; I think of you through the watches of the night.

Psalm 104:34: May my meditation be pleasing to him, as I rejoice in the LORD.

Psalm 119:15: I meditate on your precepts and consider your ways.

Psalm 119:78: May the arrogant be put to shame for wronging me without cause, but I will meditate on your precepts.

Psalm 119:148: My eyes stay open through the watches of the night that I may meditate on your promises.

His faith was so tremendous he killed a bear and a lion and finally conquered the Philistine giant Goliath, who taunted and intimidated the disarrayed army of Israel for about forty days.

9.7 Gives Access to Inspired Ideas

Meditation is one of the vital breeding grounds for inspiration. That is why Isaac went out to the field to meditate (Oyedepo, 2010). One needs to make a conscious effort to stay focused to receive ideas. And to achieve that, one also needs to invest time thinking about the subject. Jesus, during His time on earth, went to a mountain top and just sat down there. He was not praying but reasoning. Ideas are the products or art of reasoning, with evidence of added value. Time, therefore, is of the utmost essence in the school of ideas.

The more time you have for reasoning, the more insight you gain, and you command greater results. Unfortunately, the mobile phones you carry about most of the time are working against you. When an idea is coming, it rings, and the idea has flown away by the time you finish answering the call. Time is an invaluable asset. Unfortunately, most people are abusers of time. We need to stop frittering away our time on unprofitable things and invest it wisely. That is the only way to move when you go out for eight hours; you must be accountable for at least six hours. Therefore, stop spending time, and start investing it! Every time investor invariably ends up an inventor.

Thomas Edison said, "Only 5% of the human race thinks. Ten percent think they are thinking, and the remaining 85% will rather die than think." George Bernard Shaw gave the statistics 2%, 3%, and 5%, respectively. However, recent studies that provided the corresponding distribution as 5%, 15%, and 80%, respectively (Oyedepo, 2010) showed many people can still not think.

Richard Nixon said, "A true idealist pursues what his heart says is right, the way his head says it will work." Thinking is the only way to generate viable ideas, as thoughts communicate ideas. Thoughts are mental treasures but are highly volatile. If we don't quickly write them down, they disappear. An inspired idea can turn any man into the envy of his world. Think of Jacob also. It took an inspired idea to free him from the oppressive hold of Laban. He was able to dictate the color and shade of his cattle by making the strong ones mate before the rods of polar he placed in front of them in the watering troughs. Through an inspired idea, he could subdue his enemy, even though he applied it to cheat his master. Nothing in the world compares with the potency of inspired ideas.

Thinkers invent things that bring improvement. So, every time you are committed to thinking, what you are doing is programming for improvement. For instance, it used to be that the only way you could get a glass of soda was from a soda fountain. Then someone came up with the idea of bottling it. He told the Coca-Cola company that they could use his idea if they would give him a fraction of their increased sales. That minute percentage made him a millionaire.

Also, the elevator at the El Cortez Hotel in San Diego could not handle the traffic. Hence, the experts, engineers, and architects were called in. They concluded that they could put another elevator in the basement. They drew the plan, but a janitor who overheard them suggested building the elevator outside. That became the first time in the history of architecture that someone constructed an elevator outside a building.

We can and should allow ourselves to be instruments in the hand of God for improving a lot of the black race, for God is no respecter of persons, but in every nation, everyone that fears Him will get to wherever He is taking people to.

Oyedepo (2010) stated that creation is done in our spirit. As the Word is spoken, it transforms our imagination into reality. Reality does not mean tangible; rather, it means truth. It exists, and whether we can touch it or not is there. Isaac was in the habit of thinking and imagining. His success in planting and reaping a hundred folds despite the famine in the land might have resulted from the inspired ideas about God and farming.

And Isaac went out to meditate in the field at the eventide: and he lifted his eyes, saw, behold, the camels were coming. (Genesis 24:63)

9.8 Power of the Human Mind

The mind has so much power as a reservoir of information, processing information, creating, and controlling our lives.

9.8.1 Unlimited Capacity

The human mind does not work at 100% of its full capacity or potential, but just a tiny percentage of its capacity and potential. Your subconscious mind is just like a memory bank with unlimited capacity to store the data in it. It stores everything you have gone through in it and stores it permanently even if you are not aware of it. Your subconscious memory comes with virtual perfection. You might have skipped and forgotten many things that happened to you, but your subconscious mind never does. It possesses that power.

9.8.2 Information Processing

There is not in existence that we cannot do if our minds will start working at 100%. Computers are nothing compared to the human mind. In many artificial intelligence tests, it is a proven fact. It can do ten quadrillion operations per second, & supercomputers are not even closer to this speed. The nature of the mind is both straightforward and highly complex. It has infinite ways you could program it, and in today's world, the mainstream programs shaped keep you in captivity. The mind is the arbitrator of life. It is the maker and shaper of circumstances and the receiver of its own outcomes. It contains both the authority to create illusion and observe reality inside itself. As spiritual beings, men own the power of the mind and are equipped with an infinite choice. We have two parts of our brain - conscious and subconscious.

9.8.3 Creativity

If anything reaches your subconscious mind, it eventually becomes a reality. Hence, whatever you believe you can achieve. If you can imagine that you will become a billionaire, then it is possible in real life also. The most powerful minds reside in people who are always aware of what they want and move directly towards it. These minds do not get distracted and have enough power to handle a dozen multi-million companies simultaneously. All of that comes from the practice of being aware of what you want to get out of this situation right now. Bill Gates always knows what he wants whenever he does anything business-related. He always intends what *exactly* he wants before he ever enters the room. This attribute allows him and other influential minds like his to stay focused on what is truly important all the time (Oyedepo, 2010).

9.8.4 Dictates Our lives

Once the mind remains in control, you can use your mind for anything you want. There are not 100 but 60000 screens playing in your mind daily. Based on some studies, Humans have 60,000–80,000 thoughts per day.[38] If this is not enough, 80% of these thoughts are generally negative, making you feel depressed even when everything is going well in your life.

We may think that our thoughts are important and have more control over our thoughts, but the reality is that as many as 98 percent of them are the same. Therefore, we live our lives in loops by being controlled by our thoughts. First, our thoughts started dictating our life. Then, we associate ourselves with a bit of thought which does not even exist for more than some seconds. The good part is that our minds also produce around 100 new ideas

---

[38] Remez Sasson. https://www.successionsciousness.com/blog/inner-peace/how-many-thoughts-does-your-mind-think-in-one-hour/

every day. Now, these are the relevant thoughts, but what happens is that they disappear in the noise of other thoughts, and we lose these precious ideas.

9.9 Power of the Brain

The brain has a massive capacity of around 2.5 petabytes. Put into gigabytes, larger than the storage unit used on most phones, the average brain can hold 2,500,000 gigabytes of information (Reber, 2010).[39]

9.10 The Treasure base

The Scripture often used 'mind' and 'heart' interchangeably. In Matt. 12: 35, the Scripture states, "The good man from his inner good treasure flings forth good things, and the evil man out of his inner evil storehouse flings forth evil things." Man speaks out from what he stored in his mind. The passage refers to the mind of a man. The word 'treasure' is translated from Greek to mean a deposit, for instance, wealth (Strong, 1988). Figuratively, it means treasure. As a deposit, the mind is where one can store all manner of things like a storehouse. The mind is so elastic and extensive that it can store thousands of information. The discourse will be incomplete without reference to the great role played by the mind in information processing, coordination, and final storage. Observations are relayed to the mind and processed through the thought process. Without the mind, there will be no storage and processing. So, when the mind is defective, whatever is seen or observed will not last, and the ability to recall is lost.

The mind is a treasure base. We can exercise the mind to become creative and initiate ideas that we can subsequently convert into wealth. The general belief is that ideas rule the world, and these ideas stem from the mind. While some people think and broaden their treasure base to generate new and unique ideas, others stuff their minds (hearts) with useless thoughts that lead to destruction instead of building up. We must take good care of our mind by watering it with the Word of God, uproot the thorns that are trying to choke up the sprouting ideas, and weed out the cares of this world which incapacitate us.

Many men, women, and youth rove from one city to another in search of means of livelihood. There is nothing wrong with looking for jobs. However, a

---

[39] Reber, P. (2010). Ask the Brains in Scientific American Mind. 21, 2, 70. Doi: 10.1038/scientificamerican mind 0510-70

little thought will show that men like us created those jobs. But they decided to devote their time thinking out something for the employment of others. If we, too, can spend time thinking and planning, we can establish business enterprises to employ many jobless youths.

Again, there is a tendency for people to ignore or neglect the gifts they have and search for others. God has blessed us with the resource mind, a treasure base, and a source of immeasurable wealth to yield endless income streams if we properly harness its resources. But for this to be realized, the mind requires training and development.

9.11 Improving the Mind

To improve the mind, we need to meditate on God's Word. Meditation is a powerful tool that has great potential to improve our minds in all the four areas indicated, and the Scripture dealt with all. The Scripture stated that we should guide our mind with all diligence, for out of it are the issues of life. Therefore, we try to remove junk from it and ensure we only think wholesome thoughts. In addition, as we meditate on the Word, our minds are renewed, and we can understand better the plan of God for our lives and receive greater insight into our studies, innovations, and businesses. Also, our level of concentration increases, and we can achieve accelerated success. This aspect and other exciting issues are discussed in Part11 of this book.

Remove junks and fill them with wholesome thoughts.

The practice of meditation is a great way to achieve the mind's fullness and eternal consciousness. In addition, these practices can help you discover the hidden powers within and know yourself better. You can improve your mind in the following ways.[40]

1. Give your brain a workout
2. Don't skip the physical exercise
3. Make time for friends
4. Keep stress in check
5. Have a laugh
6. Eat a brain-boosting diet
7. Identify and treat health problems

---

[40] Smith, M., Segal, J., and Robinson, L. (2021). How to Improve Your Memory. https://www.helpguide.org/articles/healthy-living/how-to-improve-your-memory.html

8. Take practical steps to support learning and memory
9. Get enough sleep

It will improve your memory, protect your brain against degeneration, and make you healthier and more productive.

Get some sunlight: Higher levels of vitamin D in your system allow you to perform better and even slow down your brain's aging. Build strong connections: It enables you to stay healthy mentally and psychologically over the long term. So, make sure you take care of your mind well since it is wealth. Your ability to reason will improve tremendously just by reading and understanding.

Be Patient. Patience covers the will to go on when something is complex and the resilience to keep thinking even when your head tells you you can't figure it out. It is also the composure to realize that it takes time and work to gain knowledge, insight, and perspective. Think of all the greats in any field in history - Physics, Math, English, Writing, Sports: Einstein, Shakespeare, Rowling, Federer — all worked patiently to achieve great success. Patience is as valuable as logic, if not more. The mind works best when you use it only to learn and not to show you are better than others. Ambitions and goals are necessary motivators. Your mind does better when you set goals for yourself and yourself alone; no one else.

Meditation. Daily meditation for 15 to 20 minutes, preferably in the morning hours, will enhance focus, concentration, and mental agility by bringing the mind to the present moment, otherwise constantly oscillating between past regrets and future anxieties. A turbulent mind filled with such uncontrolled thoughts drains out the energy called prana (life force energy), leaving us completely tired, exhausted, and frustrated. Meditation prepares the mind to calm down effortlessly.

The power of the mind lies in the subconscious mind. This houses all the events, feelings, emotions, and beliefs since conception in the womb and throughout our lives. We also have a conscious mind, the one we think, calculate, reason, and act with. We use it every day. We get results because of what we do, which is determined by how we think, and our thinking is driven by our subconscious programming our belief system.

To reprogram the subconscious to get the results we want, we need to access it through the conscious mind. We should always focus on what we want, not what we do not want. We need to facilitate this reprogramming by using affirmations, visualization, conscious thinking, and feelings.

Perhaps you find it challenging to tarry and wait on God patiently, unlike Mary Magdalene until you obtain a revelation. Or you feel your mind is always troubled that you cannot receive any message. Yet, no matter your human limitations, God can rise above them and endue you with His favor and every earthly blessing in abundance. "And God is able to make all grace (every favor and earthly blessing) come to you in abundance, so that you may always and under all circumstances and whatever the need be self-sufficient (possessing enough to require no aid or support and furnished in abundance for every good work and charitable donation" (II Cor. 9:8).

CHAPTER TEN

CALL UPON HIM

10.1 Introduction

Behold, before they call, I will answer, and while they are still talking, I will reply. That is a great promise of God to His children. God wants to satisfy our needs according to His riches in glory by Christ Jesus. He is waiting for us to call his name, and as soon as we begin to do so, He will answer. God is interested in our happiness. He is not wicked as many, and the devil will try to paint Him simply because they do not pray in line with His will, and they want Him to rubber-stamp their requests. Even though He is eager to answer us, it does not mean He will respond when the prayer is outside His will for us. There are many reasons He will answer — His loving-kindness, His forever-enduring mercy endures forever, His covenant, His words, and His Son Jesus.

10.2 His Son Jesus

The case of blind Bartimaeus comes to mind. Despite the crowd around him and his schedule, Jesus waited as soon as He heard his voice. Jeremiah 33:3 is an invitation to us by God to call upon God, and He will show us great and mighty things which we do not know. According to the Amplified Version of the Bible, those 'great and mighty things' are fenced and hidden. We do not know them. We do not distinguish and recognize them; we do not have knowledge and understanding of what they are; yet, they are great and mighty.

In Hebrew, Great and mighty is Gadowl, gaw-dole (Strongs, 1988), which means great, aloud, exceedingly far. Oxford Advanced Learners Dictionary defines 'great' as Very big, much bigger than average in size and quantity (Hornby, 2015). The word 'mighty' is used to describe someone very strong and powerful; of a large and impressive thing. So, God is inviting us to call upon Him, and He will show us those things that are large, impressive, and exceedingly beyond our comprehension and knowledge, we do not know. It could be in the area of our ministries, academics, businesses, inventions, and so on. It is not only one thing but many.

What is the essence of the revelation? One of the aims is to raise us above our fellows, honor us, and show the world that we are peculiar, unique, and priceless to Him. It shows we are unique to Him, the apple of His eyes.

Many Christians can do every other thing apart from calling on God in humility for revelation and guidance. Failure in life and in all works of life could result from a lack of revelation. A company can maintain superiority and have a competitive edge if it is resourceful and inventive. God can sow the seed of invention in us based on revelation.

A student may find it difficult to understand his subject because he has not received revelation (enlightenment) about it. When I looked back on my student days, Organic Chemistry was a challenging subject for me. I worked very hard and studied all I could in the library until I had a revelation when I called on God one day. God may leave you to spend all your efforts and fish all night without catching fish until you acknowledge your worthlessness and inadequacies. God is "able to do exceedingly abundantly above all that we ask or think, according to the power that works in us" (Eph. 3:20 KJV). "He who did not withhold or spare (even) His own Son but gave Him up for us all, will He not also with Him freely and graciously give us all (other) things? (Rom. 8:32).

One day, I went to my wardrobe and thought in my heart, "I would like to own a blue shirt."

I went to work that same day and forgot all about my thoughts. That same day, my former master's student and another man, a pastor I had never seen before, visited me in my office.

I offered them seats. After the usual greetings, the pastor, who I had never met before, said God ministered to him to bless me. Dashing downstairs to his car, he rushed back and handed a gift to me. I opened it. To my surprise, it contained a blue shirt - the exact color I had desired that morning! A joyful song sang in my heart. 'So, that Scripture is very true? God, I thank you,' I mumbled as my visitors stood up and left. They did not stay long. I think God wanted to show me what that Scripture meant. He wanted to show me He could do something I think in my heart. He is gracious and willing to grant us what we think and ask. This is why we should guide our hearts (minds) with all diligence, for out of it are the issues of life. What exactly do you think in your heart? Are they defeatist thoughts full of bitterness and wrath that paralyze and stifle the life in you or wholesome and faith-full thoughts that edify and invigorate life?

If God can do far exceedingly more than we think or pray, He can also do great and mighty things we never think or dream of. Call upon Him.

10.3 Innovation through Revelation

The Scripture presented several cases of innovations and inventions right from the Book of Genesis to Revelation. God demonstrated His creative powers when He declared, "Let there be light," and there was light. Next, He created the heavens and the earth, the animal world, the living organisms in the seas, and the birds of the air. God made those things through the creative power of His words. He has faith in His words – He calls those things that appear as if they already exist. Yes, of course, they exist in His mind. He calls them up from His minds, His thoughts.

In Genesis chapter 6, the human on earth followed His pattern, even though for the wrong purpose, just as several people used the mind to create evil and started building a tower that would reach heaven. They succeeded until God confused them because their motive was wrong.

In Exodus 2, Moses was born. To protect him from the sinister law of Pharaoh, which decreed death to every male child born of a Hebrew woman, they constructed a little ship craft from papyrus to make it watertight. The material was light and prevented Moses from sinking until Pharaoh's daughter picked and adopted him. The technology exhibited in the design and construction of the ship craft is akin to what shipbuilders use in the construction of modern shipbuilding.

Another exciting part of the innovation exhibited by Miriam and her mother was how they planned Moses' protection from the mighty army of Pharaoh that was lurking all over the place to seize and kill the children born by the Israeli women. They knew that the only way to save Moses was to deliver him into Pharaoh's daughter's warm and protective arms. God gave them the wisdom. The very person Pharaoh wanted to destroy dined and wined in Pharaoh's house and learned all the Science and Arts of Egypt. That is what God can do. He could use the enemy to raise His soldiers, where necessary. How unsearchable His knowledge!

We have another interesting case in the book of Genesis, Chapter 21, verse 19. "And God opened her eyes, and she saw a well of water."

Abraham had just sent Hagar away with his son, Ishmael, according to God's instruction. As Hagar wandered in the wilderness, she missed her way. The water she had in the bottle for her and her son was gone. The child started weeping. She raised the bottle and allowed the last drop to trickle down his patchy throat. It couldn't quench his thirst. He cried all the more.

Hagar's stomach hardened as she focused on what to do to provide water for him. Pinching her lips together, she ran her hands through her hair, pacing in short spans with a jerky movement. She wondered a little distance away, staring at the dunes. Then, having found no solution, she sat opposite the child and began to groan theatrically. The child, too, cried. Then, the Lord heard their cries and opened her eyes to see a pool of water.

It was miraculous. It was not very certain the water was there initially; otherwise, she would have seen it. In response to her prayers and the child's tears, God opened her eyes. God did two things. He created the pool of water, and secondly, He opened her eyes to see it.

It is also possible that the water could be available, yet one would not see it. How often have I read a verse in the Scripture without noticing the water of life? The reason is that until one's eyes are opened, one will not see the hidden Word of God. We all need to cry to God like Hagar often to see the revelation in the Word. Only as the Lord opens our eyes will we behold wondrous things out of His Word. In His light shall we see the light. In order words, as our inner eyes are opened, we can see the gem in His Word.

Many people study or read the Scriptures without benefiting from it, like Hagar. They are thirsty. They have taken the last drop of water of life. All hope is gone. But God, the great provider who has promised to supply all our needs according to His riches in Christ Jesus, is concerned. He will never leave you nor forsake you. Can a maiden forget her necklace? Can a mother forget her sucking child? Yes, even if she does, as we have witnessed in times of war, God will not. We are engraved in the palms of His hands. Call upon Him, and He will open your eyes to see the pool of water.

10.4 Enlarging Our Minds for Innovation - Come Apart and Rest

Human beings naturally have an adventurous spirit and want to explore things. Mountain climbing is one such activity where people exercise themselves regularly. Mountain climbing has several advantages to the body, mind, and social life.

Health-wise, mountain climbing is very beneficial to your body. It increases heart efficiency and enables it to pump blood better and lower blood pressure. The heavy breathing that goes on during mountain climbing helps maximize your lung capacity, expel air retained in the lungs, and create room for some new perspective. While causing weight loss, it tones the body while also lowering the blood sugar level. In addition, mountain climbing improves self-esteem, awareness, and creativity because it enables one to live in the present.

Certain things can prevent us from discovering and exercising our gifts and talents. Exhaustion hurts creativity. When you stay busy and do not rest, your mind is not as sharp. Technology (texting, social networking, TV, computer games) can rob creativity and steal lots of time, preventing us from strengthening our talents. Another big creativity blocker is pride. Talent is a gift, so thank God for the ideas and talents He has given you and uses them to glorify Him.

10.4.1 Social Life

According to psychologist Tim Lahaye, Moses had low self-esteem, a character trait associated with the melancholy group. So, could God had desired to improve his self-esteem by constantly asking him to come up to the mountain?

Moses went up on Mount Sinai several times to meet God, as recorded in Exodus 19 through the end of the book. Moses climbed Mt. Sinai about eight times to meet with the Lord depending on the reckoning.[41] One can follow the two different routes to reach the top: the camel track (ascent takes 2.5-3 hours up). The camel track is a less tasking route, and certainly, riding a camel reduces the climbing strain, but probably not the riding sores. The 3700 steps (ascent takes 1.5-2 hours, the descent takes 1 hour). Probably, at the time of Moses, no one had created the steps, and he did not climb using a camel.

---

[41] Page 116 Section 10.4.1 paragraph 2 line 3- https://www.gotquestions.org/Moses-on-Mount-Sinai.html

The climb of a height of 2,285 m up and another 2,285 m down[42] must have fully exercised his muscles and distracted him from administrative, judicial, and executive demands of governing. It must have been a refreshing retreat and quiet time for him when he sat silently at the foot of God to receive revelations and instructions.

Mountain climbing is a sport that will force you to live in a basic form for the period the activity lasts, and this will only make you appreciate some things in this life that you might have taken for granted. It also increases your blood oxygen levels or the amount of oxygen carried by your blood to different parts of your body. Uphill and brisk walking has also reduced chronic illnesses, such as heart disease, type 2 diabetes, asthma, stroke, and even some cancers (Gardner, 2014). Among the numerous physical benefits, Pete[43] mentioned that mountain climbing could improve sleep.

10.4.2 Improves Leadership Skills

As a leader, Moses needed to learn how to organize himself better, plan better and keep time. He required all manner of skills – reflective cognitive and deductive skills, which are very important for his success. While enjoying nature and the beauty that comes with it, God might have planned to create an uncontrolled environment for building these leadership skills. In addition, people who have melancholy character traits enjoy nature. God knows the needs of every man as the creator. God might have invited him severally up the mount to improve his heart performance, lungs circulation, and lower blood pressure. This is not to demean God's miraculous power. Such intense aerobic activity can increase the capacity of your lungs via heavy breathing and clear the residual air from your lungs with fresher air (Gardner, 2014).

It was a great leadership challenge to lead and direct thousands of people, especially when they are stubborn, faithless, and unteachable. God must have felt inviting him to the mountains to calm his body, allow him to rest, and eliminate all stress.

"You have stayed in this mountain for too long." The primary lesson to be derived from the above passage is the lesson of one launching us for a higher purpose and not allowing past achievements to dull our desire for something greater.

---

[42] https://www.memphistours.com/Egypt/
https://wikitravel.org/en/Mount-Sinai
[43] https://www.mountkenyaadventures.com/benefits-of-mountain-climbing/

In addition, Moses, being melancholy, might have found the incredible sight of the mountain top, which allows him a panoramic view of the surrounding regions, very exhilarating that he was no longer eager to lead the people for a while. So, no matter how wonderful the present experience is, one must understand that there are still mighty and plentiful things to see and know. We can never know God exhaustively, for He is omniscient.

10.2.4 Boosts Self Confidence

People who have melancholic character traits lack self-confidence. Mountaineering can increase confidence as one reaches the top since it takes courage and perseverance to achieve this fit, depending on the height of the mountain. Reaching the summit after a trying moment is euphoric. Earning such panoramic views can induce a euphoric sense of accomplishment.

10.2.5 Increases Focus and Attention

Mountaineering is associated with "Attention Restoration Theory" (ART) which characterizes two types of attention: directed and involuntary. We use directed attention when doing computer work and are best recharged through involuntary attention. One way of stimulating the directed attention is by viewing beautiful natural settings and mountain landscapes which humans need to feel good (Griffiths, 2013). Seeing a far distance without obstruction, like trees or shrubs, is refreshing for attentiveness. God wanted Moses's absolute attention during that mountain experience when he was alone with God, away from the bustles of life and away from multitudes of irritating, stubborn, and faithless people. The more expansive the view, with the most clarity and the least amount of obstruction, the more refreshing for attentiveness and well-being the experience is.

10.2.6 Reduction in Anger

Climbing above the tree line offers breathtaking vantage points with a vast unobstructed view due to the lack of vegetation. Psychologists Gatersleben and Andrews (2013) discovered that this type of environment causes emotions of sadness to decrease dramatically and anger to diminish substantially. God might have chosen the mountain site as the best location to pass some crucial information to Moses because of another therapeutic reason - to reduce his tendency to be angry.

However, in 'low prospect high refuge' environments like a dense forest, anger increased, and sadness did not decrease. Further, the ability to concentrate increased substantially in 'high level of prospect and low level of refuge' compared to other landscapes, suggesting high altitude mountains are an ideal learning location.

Like most mountains, the study also states that experiencing awe evokes more profound thoughts and reflections (Griffiths, 2013).

Essentially, climbing mountains can be refreshing for your working attention; it can reset your attention span and make you a much happier person. This is greatly beneficial for one's mental health, especially in an age where most people are working stressful jobs and not exercising enough to outlet said stress.

Many studies have linked exercise to improvements in moods and mental health, and mountaineering is a complete full-body exercise (Chrobak, 2017). Mountaineering and spending time in nature have also been linked to aiding depression. According to some studies, climbing can be a form of therapy used for depression and other mental illnesses.

Younghee Lowry, a crisis worker in Tahoe, California, uses climbing as a type of "Mindfulness therapy," a treatment described by the American Psychological Association (APA) as "paying attention to one's experience in the present moment, observing thoughts and emotions from moment to moment without judging" (Moore, 2018).

The summary is that we need to create an enabling environment for productive and creative thinking and recharge our minds with the awesomeness of God and His creation to function maximally. Staying in the valley all day with no time for rest, caged in by crippling life circumstances without the panoramic mountain life experience can quench the flowing fire of innovation and reduce our attention to hear and receive from God the 'great and mighty things which we do not know.'

CHAPTER ELEVEN

LORD, OPEN MY EYES

11.1 Introduction

Oritzi (1975) said that "the mighty deeds of God are everywhere. Our trouble is that we do not see them." Our eyes are closed. How can we spend our days murmuring and complaining because we fail to see and appreciate the great and mighty things God is doing? When our spouses make mistakes, we forget all the good things they have done in the past. Our minds have a strong affinity towards remembering only the wrong things and magnifying them too. If our eyes are opened to see the beauty of the flowers in the garden, the birds that wake us up with their chattering, and other works of God's hand, the so-called big mountains of the vicissitude of life will come crashing down under the shouts of praise. And we will be better Christians. When I consider the heavens, the work of your hands, the moon and the stars you have ordained, what is a man that you think of him? And the son of man, that you care for him? (Psalm 8: 3, 4).

After the resurrection of Jesus, He appeared to two of his disciples going to Emmaus. They walked with Jesus for several kilometers, hearing His voice without recognizing Him (The Gospel of Luke 24:13-35). That continued until He opened their eyes. Their experience underscores the importance of having one's eyes opened to understand Jesus and appreciate His teachings and dealings with us. Then, the disciples could look back after the revelation and say, "No wonder. That was why our hearts were burning. That was why His words were cutting through our hearts like a two-edged sword."

If He had not opened their eyes, they would not have recognized Him despite His being with them. His words would not have had the intended impact if they had not realized the one who was with them. The extent one regards and accepts an expression made by a person depends, among other factors, on the person's personality and the respect and faith the hearer has for the speaker. It is a function of the perception of the knowledge and experience of the speaker by the hearer. So, we need our eyes opened to understand who is speaking to us in church. In church, people often see the man at the pulpit and not the Spirit speaking through Him. Hence, they do not receive the words, and it makes no impact on their lives. Some become engrossed with the grammatical mistakes or exactitude of the comments and sentences, physical structure, architectural beauty, demonstrations, and pulpit gymnastics that they fail to recognize who is speaking. We need to ask God one thing Lord open my eyes to see Jesus through the preacher.

Another lesson is that it is possible to be in church, hear all the words, stay two hours in service, go through the religious rituals, and yet not recognize Jesus. Could it be why we go to church, hear all the messages, and go back the same because our spiritual eyes are blind?

Walking speeds can vary greatly depending on many factors such as height, weight, age, terrain, surface, load, culture, effort, and fitness. However, the average human walking speed at crosswalks is about 5.0 kilometers per hour (km/h), or about 1.4 meters per second (m/s), or about 3.1 miles per hour (mph).[44] From Jerusalem to Emmaus was 10.4 to 12 km.[45] The two disciples of Jesus were involved in a conversation for a distance of 11 km. An average person walks at 5 Km per hour. And when people discuss as they walk, the speed reduces. But if we take this conservative rate, they spent 2 hours 12 minutes with Jesus, yet they did not know Him because their eyes were not open. Some church services last about two and a half hours. That explains why so many people listen, laugh at jokes, sing, clap, and yet do not recognize Jesus. We need to ask God to open our eyes.

It is baffling that these men were called Jesus disciples. That means they knew him to a certain extent. It will not be farfetched if one thinks they had

---

[44] Zyl, L.V. (2015). Fit and Proper: What is the ideal Walking speed for you? Business standard. https://www.business.standard.com/article-currentaffairs/fit-proper-what_is-the-ideal-walking-speed-for-you115100900029_1.html.

[45] https://Israelbibletours.ca/destinations/emmaus/https://religion.fandom.com

been with Jesus. They had sacrificed much for His kingdom. They had accepted Him as their master. They used to take their cross daily and follow Him. They used to deny themselves. They were doing all those things the Scriptures say that one cannot be His disciple if one does not do. Yet, they failed to recognize Him. We need to pray, 'Lord, open our eyes.'

How often do we fail to recognize Jesus in our lives - His workings, miracles, his words? How often we are carried away by the message and forget to recognize the voice of our Lord. Perhaps they were so overwhelmed by the stories about Jesus' resurrection around that time.

They were not open and transparent. They felt something - the unction of the Holy Spirit the same others felt when they said, "No one ever spoke like Him," yet, they bottled up their feelings. Some Christians are so tied up that they cannot confess Jesus to anyone. They cannot even express how the Lord has impacted them.

11.2. See God's Promise

It is not enough reading or even studying God's promises. We often read them and sometimes study them. But unless we see the promises, i.e., our eyes are open, we can't know them. We need revelation. In Heb. 11: 13, Abraham and other men of God saw the promises from a long way off and welcomed them. It was through revelation. Jesus had not come and died, but God opened their eyes to understand God's purpose and will for humankind. They had not the advantages we have. We could draw close and see from a very close range because the Wall of partition had been broken, and the Holy Spirit is dwelling in our hearts. We have been drawn closer to behold the Word of life.

Heb. 11: 14 says, "they were looking for a country of their own, a country not made with hands eternal in the heavenly places." What we are looking for determines our direction and our focus. It concerns our aim and goals, and visions in life. It makes one remain focused. What are we looking for? What do we have our eyes peeled to?

Love not to sleep, lest you come to poverty; open your eyes, and you will be satisfied with bread. (Pr.20:13)

The Hebrew word used here, Paquach, means "to open the senses, especially the eyes." Figuratively, it means to be observant. Sometimes Christians grope about in darkness over some issues in their lives. Job creation opportunities abound around them, which they are ignorant of. They have lived in the same state of joblessness for years. Sometimes they think their problem is a lack of money to start up a business or even a lack of opportunities. But the major problem is that their eyes are closed to see some of the economically viable ventures they can embark on. They are not observant. Their focus and lopsided preoccupation only with specific jobs and opportunities have blindfolded them.

Then, one day in the same place that seemed shrouded in darkness, where there are no opportunities, someone comes up with a wonderful idea. They will wonder how such an opportunity has eluded them. So, may God open your eyes so that your days of languishing in poverty will be over.

Another related verse in the Scripture is Ps. 119:18; "Open my eyes, that I may behold wondrous things out of your law." The 'Law' in this sense denotes 'scripture.' The Scripture is full of wondrous things. But it is only as we rely on the Holy Spirit when we study the Word that we will behold these wondrous things. The Hebrew word for 'open' 'galah' used here has several shades of meanings: reveal, disclose, discover, open plainly, and so on. The Scripture is so rich and powerful with sources of enablement and empowerment. The gem in the Word of God is usually hidden and fenced to the person who the devil blinds. A Christian who is not diligent in looking at the Word carefully will not see the wondrous things. As we pick the Bible and begin to study it, we should always come with open minds and ask God to open our eyes to behold the great things which will help us live as better Christians.

The same Word was used in 2 Kings 6:17, 20. Through the Word of Knowledge, Elisha, the prophet, always knew the plans of the King of Syria ahead of time to attack the King of Israel and He revealed them to him later. This infuriated the king of Syria, and he sent his army to capture Elisha. The army contingent surrounded the house of Elisha at night. His servant saw the soldiers in horses and chariots and was terrified and cried, 'Alas, my master! What shall we do?" Elisha said, "Fear not, for those with us are more than those with them." Then, he prayed that God should open his servant's eyes to see the army of the Lord of Host round about them. The army was not only equipped with horses and chariots but with horses and chariots of fire. The main interest here is in the use of the word 'open' and what happened when Gehazi's eyes were opened.

Firstly, God can open our eyes to see the supernatural things or beings around us. The purpose might be to comfort and strengthen our faith. Secondly, all around us are God's protective angels if we are indeed his children. It can be comforting if we realize that, especially when we are under attack from the enemy. Finally, we can always ask God to open our eyes to see into the supernatural. God may choose to do that by allowing us to glimpse it physically, through a vision or dream, or more importantly, through the scriptures. That will bring comfort to our souls.

As I began to embark on a series of journeys across the country to raise money for my family, one of my wife's great revelations was about a hefty armed man who was accompanying me wherever I went. It strengthened my faith in God that He is by my side and will always protect me from accidents and evil men that operate on highways.

I remember a particular case I was in a hotel in Owerri. I was woken by a bang on the door and a loud noise coming from an opposite room at night. The next adjacent door was kicked open. I knew it was robbers who were in operation from the noise around. So, I began to pray and turned into a prayer warrior. They came to mine after robbing the two rooms, turned the doorknob, and went away. I was told in the morning that they made away with laptops and an expensive camera from the guests in those two opposite rooms. In addition, they took away a lot of cash from the hotel and beat up the security men and the receptionist.

We don't always see the invisible army unless God decides to let us enjoy that privilege in his divine choice. But whether He allows us to see them or not, we should rest assured they are always around us, watching over us.

When we do not see things the way God sees them, we are bound to misjudge His silence or delay as a lack of love and give up hope of patiently waiting for dawn. If only God would open our eyes to see the wondrous things he is arranging for us; if only we would understand that He who began with us will bring us to the expected end and that He will never abandon us halfway (Akanni, 2002).

11.3 Revelation of the Riches of Christ

The revelation of the Riches of Christ can make one understand how mighty our riches in glory by Christ Jesus is; no one will understand this and remain faithless. Sometimes, Christians are like the Israelites, who saw themselves as grasshoppers. We are affected by the way we see ourselves. God may touch us to begin to see ourselves the way God sees us. We not only need to see the deprivations and wickedness in our lives which will drive us to God, but we also need to see what Christ has done for us, which will enable us to mount on our heavenly position to sit on God's right hand.

11.4 Revelation of His glory

Stephen was one of the twelve deacons selected to organize the distribution of food among the disciples of Jesus when the Hellenists (the Greek-speaking Jews) spoke against the native Jews because their widows were being overlooked and neglected in the daily ministration (distribution) of relief (Act 6:1). He was a man full of faith and the Holy Spirit. He worked great wonders and miracles in the synagogue, full of divine blessing and favor and power. Nevertheless, the Jews conspired against and framed him and brought him before the Sanhedrim. As he began to defend himself, accusing their ancestors of stubbornness and persecution of prophets, they were infuriated. Stephen gazed up and saw the glory of God and Jesus standing at His right hand. It was a great revelation (Acts 6: 55, 56). The Scripture said that Jesus is seated at God's right hand. It might mean that Jesus was so excited about this His son who stood boldly for what he believed stood up. He allowed him to glimpse His glory and, in fact, stood up as if He was cheering him proudly and about to receive him home.

First, we noticed that Stephen was full of the Holy Spirit. So, it was not surprising he saw into the realm of the Spirit. This was the third time it was mentioned that he was full of the Holy Spirit (Acts 6: 3, 5, 8; 7:55). The Spirit searches all things, and he is the revealer. Stephen had a foretaste of the throne of God. This revelation must have strengthened him to withstand the physical torture and death by stoning. We are seated together with Christ in the heavenly places. If we should draw an analogy from the earthly kingdom, a son or heir does not stand up while others sit. An heir sits on a seat beside his father. So, also the image God created by the above verse. Seating is the normal position of our Lord Jesus. But in a deep respect for Stephen, the first Christian martyr, He stood up.

11.5 Revelation of Jesus

Isaiah saw God in His glory and majesty. We need to have our eyes opened to behold the majesty of God, to behold Him in all His power and glory. That was the prayer Paul prayed for the Ephesian church – that the eyes of their understanding will be opened to see the Word the way it is. We need the Holy Spirit to reveal to us the promises of God the way they are.

11.6 Revelation of Our position in Christ

We have been translated from the powers of darkness into the kingdom of light. During the new birth, a Christian is transferred out of the influence of the powers of darkness into a different kingdom. That is why the devil cannot harm him because he is operating at a different level altogether. He is in Christ in whom he moves and has his being.

The Word of God said we should be transformed by the renewing of our mind. Rom. 12:2 says, "Do not be conformed to this world (this age), (fashioned after and adapted to its external, superficial customs), but be transformed (changed) by the (entire) renewal of your mind (by its new ideals and its new attitude) so that you may prove (for yourselves) what is the good and acceptable and perfect will of God, even the thing which is good and acceptable and perfect (in His sight for you)"

Mathematically, the word transformation involves translation, magnification, rotation, and inversion. To facilitate the solution of a mathematical problem, the problem solver maps or transforms the problem from one plane to another. In the old plane, the problem is difficult to solve. On the other hand, in the new plane, the problem loses some of its characteristics, making it easier to solve. The transformation can involve translation, which is a change in position; magnification, which is an increase in magnitude; or rotation, which is an alteration in orientation, and inversion, which means a total change in configuration. Initiation of transformation starts as soon as someone is born again.

11.6.1 Translation

First, his dead Spirit is quickened so that he could connect to God and receive the things of the Spirit. Simultaneously, he is placed in Christ, and his life becomes hidden in Christ and in God to ensure his protection from the devil's onslaught (Col. 1:13; 3:1). The location in Christ is an enviable and blessed one – we are seated together with Him at the right hand of God, a place of authority, joy, and righteousness forever (Ps.48: 10). From that vantage position, the principalities and powers are made subject to us.

Placing a Christian in Christ or his being transferred from the powers of darkness into the kingdom of heaven involves an aspect of spiritual transformation called "translation." In Mathematics, it involves lateral displacement from the original position to another. In other words, the new birth requires the movement of the believer from the place where the powers of darkness reigned supreme into the kingdom of God (In Christ) where peace, joy, and righteousness are the hallmark. That explains why the devil cannot molest believers who understand their rights and privileges. They fail to see him when they come one way to harm him because his life is hidden in Christ. They run away seven ways because the arm of the Lord is revealed, and they cannot just stand before Him.

11.6.2 Magnification

The new birth also involves magnification. In Christ, the believer's abilities are magnified through the abundant grace showered on Him by the Lord Jesus Christ. "For out of His fullness (abundance) we have all received (all had a share and we were all supplied with) one grace after another and spiritual blessing upon spiritual blessing and even favor upon favor and gift (heaped) upon gift." (Jn. 1:16). God has richly blessed us with spiritual blessings, favors, and gifts. How can someone be blessed to such an extent and remain bankrupt of ideas? He is empowered to do and achieve more. Paul said, "I can do all things through Christ who strengthens me." A believer is enabled to do more than he could ordinarily do when he was an unbeliever. The Holy Spirit who lives in Him now, who is greater than the hordes of demons outside, the Ebenezar, standby, advocate, helper, and intercessor, through His various unique ministries in him, enables him to achieve more, not only in terms of magnitude but also in quality. One of our major problems is a refusal to involve Him in our plans and activities or ignorance of His invigorating working power in us who believe.

11.6.3 Rotation

In addition, the believer undergoes a type of transformation called 'rotation.' His orientation and viewpoint are affected as he begins to alter his priorities. Certain things may no longer be as important. Heavenly goals and attainment of success in spiritual matters become his focus as he sets his affection on the things above, not on the things below (Col. 3:1). His thinking pattern changes, and he emphasizes the essential things in his life. Some Christians are criticized as soon as they become believers because their attitudes become affected. Some even drop their old friends and change their visions and goals in life. There is disorientation. It could be subtle, like a slight shift in the angular inclination of a line, or very pronounced, as a rotation of

180 degrees. Another form of transformation is inversion. The first three transformations make up what is called a linear transformation.

11.6.4 Inversion

Linear transformation plus inversion gives bilinear transformation. According to the Cambridge English Dictionary' Inversion' is a situation in which something is changed so that it is the opposite of what it was before, or something is turned upside down. The Jews said to the Christians, "...the people who turn the world upside down have come." Christianity may involve doing things the opposite way the custom and societal norms demand. The Lord Jesus defiled the Sabbath and worked some miracles during a Sabbath day instead of resting. That was an inversion. Different applications of the Word to many disciplines are explained in Collins's English Dictionary. Mathematically, it is a transformation that takes a point P to a point P1 such that OP.OP1 = a2 where a is a constant and P and P1 lie on a straight line through a fixed-point O and on the same side.

A Christian may exhibit an attitude that is a direct opposite to the societal norm because of his new belief system. While physically there are no changes, there are changes wrought by the Holy Ghost inside of him. He may look exactly how he used to look, walk with the same gait, and have the same distinctive mannerism, yet his whole attitude regarding some actions, preferences, and desires is the direct opposite of what they used to be.

11.5.5 Essence of transformation

What is the essence of the whole transformation, one may ask? First, of course, it is to redeem the believer from spiritual death, animate and espouse him to Christ, begat other children for God, and so on. But one of the primary reasons from the viewpoint of our discourse is to make it easier for him to obey God and live like Christ. In order words, to enable him to be conformed to the image of Christ, to restore the image of man which was lost in the garden of Eden when Adam sold out through compromise.

In mathematics, the essence of transformation is to map a problem from one place to another, which changes the characteristics of the problem such that it becomes easy to solve. For instance, Laplace transformation will map a differential equation from a time (t) plane to a complex s plane. As a result, the differential equation becomes an algebraic equation that is far simpler to solve. The problem is solved in the s – plane and then back-transformed into the original (t) plane to give the solution in terms of t. This is the general principle of many transformations in mathematics – always to simplify the problem. Let us apply this once again to the spiritual life of a Christian.

There are two planes, spiritual and physical, with different characteristics. God understood our frailties as humans placed under the physical planet. He gave us a set of laws to guide us, but the laws could not help us become like Him. It only made us more conscious of our weaknesses and susceptibility to sin. We could not achieve any spiritual progress or success. We had the devil, our flesh, and weak mind all fighting against us. So, God decided to move us into another plane where our problem will be solved quickly, under a platform that will enable us to live like Christ, where we can operate by grace and satisfy the demands of the Holy God, in Christ where grace operates. Jesus said, "Come unto me all you that labor and are heavily laden, and I will give you rest. Take upon you my yoke is easy, and the burden is light. Learn of me, and you will find rest for your soul." (Mt. 11: 28 - 29). The believer can in the new plane live holy. "Sin shall have no dominion over you for you are not under the law but under grace." (Rom. 6:11, 14). "For there is now no condemnation to those in Christ Jesus, who walk not after the law but after the spirit. For the law of the spirit has set us free from the law of sin and death" (Rom 8:1, 2).

The mapping or transformation technique or instrument is the Word of God.

God uses the Word of God to transform us. As we study the Word of God and open our hearts to it, our minds are renewed, and we become transformed and more conformable to the image of Christ. A renewed mind finds it hard to practice sin. He is fortified, and his Spirit is strengthened to resist the devil. In that sense, the transformation is a continuous exercise, daily beholding ourselves in the mirror of the Word; daily gathering and eating the manna for our spiritual sustenance until we come to full maturity, until we conform completely to his image at the close of the age when we shall see Him and be exactly as He is.

CHAPTER TWELVE

GREAT STEPS FOR RECEIVING REVELATIONS

12.1 Great Revelations

Great revelations, as we learned above, are fenced in and hidden. They are not for the faint or undetermined fellows. They are hidden treasures that only those willing to search for them will find. They are enclosed and can only be reached by those who take the pains to scale over the gigantic fences. Jesus said, "Ye search the scriptures for they testify of me..." We need to search the scriptures. The scriptures show us who Christ is, what he did and does, why he is, etc. As we explore the scriptures, we know Him as our unlimited source of strength, power, might, and everything. For without Him, we are nothing.

When Mary Magdalene went to Jesus' grave to anoint His body, her action revealed how one can receive great revelation. Mary Magdalene left early in the morning and went to the grave. A harsh dry wind blew across her puffy eyes. For three days since the burial of the Lord, she could not sleep as poignant thoughts gnawed at her mind. She wrinkled her brows, wondering how she would remove the heavy stone covering the grave. *I forgot, I should have told Peter to go with me,* she thought. Then, as she approached the site, she did a double-take. "Thank God, it is open. Someone has already opened it," she smiled.

Peter and John, the disciples of Jesus, overtook her.

Peter jumped into the grave and moved inside. "This was exactly where he was laid." His eyes popped out of his head as he saw the grave cloth carefully wrapped and placed on the pillow position. He glanced around the grave and peered at the cloth again, rubbing his eyes. What he saw earlier did not change. Rooted to the spot, he lingered for a while and then dashed out. The other disciples stared at him.

"Did you see him?"

"No." He shook his head, folding his arm across his chest. "His body is not there. They've taken him away."

"It is not possible." Mary Magdalene rubbed at an eyelid. "I saw Joseph of Arimathea take His body from the soldiers and bury Him in the tomb."

"You can check for yourself. He is not there."

"This is serious." Her throat thickened.

Peter stood staring at the ground, trying to figure out what might have happened to Him. Then, he walked to her. "Let us leave here. Perhaps the Chief Priest has taken Him away."

"Where?" Magdalene asked.

"Let us go."

"Leave me alone." She hissed. "I'm not going anywhere until I see Him."

He gaped at her. "Wipe your tears and let us leave. It's not safe for you to stay alone here." He frowned as he swept a glance around. "We shall inform the other disciples and decide what to do about it."

"Please, Peter, go away. I'll remain here."

After a fruitless attempt to persuade her to follow them back to the city, he left her and went away. But Mary Magdalene waited. Her love for Jesus cast away the fear of seeing ghosts, madmen who roomed around tombs, and being raped by criminals. She waited. She was determined she must see Jesus. Nothing will dissuade her. She was interested in one thing – to see Jesus.

12.1 She remained

Mary Magdalene remained. While others were confused about what happened to His body and left in discouragement, she waited. She had one aim in mind. She had one desire. It was to see Jesus. So much in our Christian race is dependent on persistence, focus, and the ability to wait. Hence, Jesus taught about importunity in prayer-men ought always to pray and not to faint. Elijah persisted until the rain fell. Getting revelation is not for the faint-hearted. If one must get revelation, he must be ready to wait on the Lord, on

His knees, to hear what the Lord has to say. He should not be in a hurry to leave His presence. Mary Magdalene's love overcame her fears of the Jews, fear of the Roman soldiers, and fear of ghosts who might jump out from the graves around her. That was an example to demonstrate that perfect love casts away fear.

12.2 She stooped low

Stooping low is a mark of humility. Revelation is not for the proud. God is far from them. He has nothing to do with them. Nevertheless, her action connotes several positive attitudes, such as humility, curiosity, and interest.

Humility is very crucial for one to receive revelation from God. God knows the pride from afar. He will never come near him, needless of revealing His mind to him. As far as God is concerned, what is awaiting him is destruction, and it is only the message of repentance he can receive from God. We must come to God in humility, knowing that without Him, we are nothing. No man can understand the Word or contact the Spirit behind the Word without the help of the Holy Spirit. If you want a revelation, you have to humble yourself before God, and He will exalt you and show you great things you do not know.

Another vital attitude is curiosity. Mary was interested in seeing the Lord. Her high interest motivated her to remain when others had gone. Sometimes we will not receive revelation because of a lack of interest. We may show interest for just a few minutes, but whoever will receive many revelations should have a persevering interest. The interest will result in curiosity and a great desire to find explanations for the missing link. Interest will awaken the desire to know more about the Word of God.

12.3 She looked

Getting revelation depends on if someone will go out of his way to look. A continuous look at the perfect law of liberty, the scriptures, is essential for God revealing things to us. Waiting is not enough. Humility is not all that is required. You have to do something about the revelation you are seeking for. It could be in academics or business or God's will generally. You must work. Pick up your Bible or book. Do not just remain idle. Begin to do something. Study so you can receive approval from God. Act. If you believe, you must act. Faith without works is dead. Do not be discouraged by a long period of reading and studying without 'catching any fish'. It is time to cast the net again and draw a net full of fishes.

12.4 She saw

One can look at the scriptures without revelation. We need the Holy Spirit to teach us to open our eyes to behold wondrous things from His Word. Magdalene peered around the same place as did Peter and John. Peter and John saw nothing. Their eyes were not opened to see beyond the grave clothes. They saw only the physical. How often do we study the Bible without digging out the gem buried simply because our eyes are not open? Two persons can read the same verse of the scriptures and get different revelations. As God's mind is unsearchable, His Word and revelations from it also are. We will not have revelation from the scriptures until God shines His light on our minds.

12.5 She heard

At last, Mary's patience bore some fruits. She heard the Lord speak to her. Can you imagine the liquid joy that must have immersed her heart when the Lord not only appeared but spoke to her? That results from patiently waiting for the Lord to give a revelation or show us something unique about Himself, the world, or the church. It is uplifting, captivating, and fulfilling. It makes Christianity more real when we hear God speak to us. Of course, many people would want to see Jesus and listen to Him speak as He spoke to Mary. But God has several ways He speaks to us, and to me, what matters is that He speaks and we hear Him. The way and manner He choose to do it is quite irrelevant.

CONCLUSION

God wants to reveal things to you as His dear child. The Scripture declares that because of the intense love He has for us, Christ, His only, sinless begotten son, tasted death for every man. You might have been dwelling in ignorance and living a life of frustration and defeat because you have not asked God to show you great and mighty things you do not know about your academics, family, business, ministry, etc. I dare you today to call upon Him. Ask Him to open your eyes or give you some ideas on how to solve your problems. His speaking or revealing a word into your circumstance will bring testimonies to you. He has created you to be creative, and you can bring life again to your dead program or company. He has given me wonderful research and innovative ideas that helped me progress in my academics to attain the zenith of my career. He has also given me some ideas to prosper in other areas. I still believe Him for more. What of you? "And the Lord opened her eyes."

REFERENCES

Akanni, G. (2002). The resurrection and the life are here. Peace House Publications. Gboko, Nigeria.

Alice G. Walton, A.G. (2012). Your Body's Internal Clock and How It Affects Your Overall Health https://www.theatlantic.com/health/archive/2012/03/your-bodys-internal-clock-and-how-it-affects-your-overall-health/254518/

Arrington, C. (2011). Creativity from God. CLUBHOUSE Jr. https://www.clubhousemagazine.com/en/extras/creativity-from-god.aspx

Buzan, T. (1972). The Ultimate Book of Mind Maps. Spore One – Structure in Hyperspace. ISBN 0-85115-016-0.

Chrobak, U. (2017). Can Climbing Be Used to Treat Depression? https://www.climbing.com/news/can-climbing-be-used-to-treat-depression/

Corcoran, L. (2015). https://www.irishtimes.com/business/how-tony-buzan-used-mind-maps-to-doodle-his-way-to-millions-

De Gelder, B., Tamietto, B., Boxtel, G., Goebel, R; Sahraie, A., den Stock, J.B., Bernard Stienen, M.C., Weiskrantz. L, Pegna, A. (2008). Intact navigation skills after bilateral loss of striate cortex.Volume 18, Issue 24, Pages R1128-R1129

Dubé, M.A., Tremblay, AY, and Liu, J. (2007). Biodiesel production using a membrane reactor. Bioresour Technol, 98(3):639-47.

Drucker, P.F. (1986). Innovation and entrepreneurship. Harper, New York

Eberle, B. (1996). *Scamper: Games for Imagination Development.* Prufrock Press Inc.

Eberle, R. F. (1972). *Developing imagination through scamper.* The Journal of Creative Behavior, 6(3), 199-20

Eikenberry, K. (2008). Innovation Management. https://innovationmanagement.se/imtool-articles/eight-ways-to-generate-more-ideas-in-a-group/

Encyclopedia Britannica. (2018). Sherpa | History & Culture. [online] Available at: https://www.britannica.com/topic/Sherpa-people [Accessed 2 Mar. 2018].

Fowler, R (2017) God's Gift of Creativity http://www.rayfowler.org

Gardner, T. (2014). *Health Benefits of Climbing and Hill Walking*. BMC, 23 July 2014, www.thebmc.co.uk/health-benefits-of-climbing-and-hill-walking.

Gatersleben, B., & Andrews, M. (2013). When walking in nature is not restorative—The role of prospect and refuge. *Health & Place, 20*, 91–101 http://thecloudline.org/the-science-behind-mountain-climbing/discovered

Griffiths, T. (2013). The Science Behind Mountain Climbing. HuffPost Canada, HuffPost Canada. www.huffingtonpost.ca/tamara-griffiths/why-mountain-climbing-feels-good_b_3833370.ht.

Gordon, W.J.J. (1961) Synectics: The Development of Creative Capacity. Harper and Row, Publishers, New York, 3

Hornby, A.S. (2015). Oxford Advanced Learner's Dictionary. Oxford University Press, Oxford

Klein, S. (2014). 9 Things You Probably Didn't Know About Your Body's Internal Clock 11/02/2014 12:19 pm ET | Updated December 7, 2017. https://www.huffpost.com/entry/circadian-rhythm-daylight-saving-internal-clock-body_n_6030142

Moore, H. (2018). Climbing for Mental Health. [online] Climbing Magazine. Available at: https://www.climbing.com/people/climbing-for-mental-health/

Martin (2015) https://www.cleverism.com/18-best-idea-generation-techniques/ *Martin Saunders is a Contributing Editor for Christian Today and the Deputy CEO of Youthscape.*

Oyakhilome, C. (2007). Recreating your world. Love World Publications, Lagos, Nigeria.

Osborn, A. (1953) Applied Imagination: Principles and Procedures of Creative Problem-Solving New York: Charles Scribner's Sons.

Oyedepo, D.O. (2010). Ruling your world. Dominion Publishing House, Lagos, Nigeria.

Pegna, A. J., Khateb, A., Lazeyras, F. & Seghier, M. L. Nature Neurosci. 8, 24–25 (2004).

Robert H. Schuller, "Tough Time Never Last But Tough People Do" 96-97.

Rohrbaugh, https://www.fromhispresence.com/radical-prayer-3-wild-ideas-witty-inventions/

Rushton, W.A.H. (1975) Visual pigments and color blindness. Scientific American Vol. 232, No. 3, 64-75

Scofield, C. I. (1996). Rightly dividing the Word of truth. Loizeaux Brothers. New Jersey.

Strong, S.T.D. (1988). Strong Exhaustive Concordance of the Bible. Christian Heritage Publishing Company, Inc

Wellman J. (2015) https://www.patheos.com/blogs/christiancrier/2015/01/11/top--7-bible-verses-about-creativity-or-being-creative/

https://zdschmoll.sarahah.com

https://www.beliefnet.com/inspiration/galleries/5-inventions-that-were-god-inspired-ideas.aspx

https://revivenations.org/blog/2011/06/18/ideas/

https://www.kathyhoward.org/ created-to-be-creative/

https://www.ideatovalue.com/inno/nickskillicorn/2019/02/podcast-s2e30-scott-kirsner-turning-innovation-management-in-to-a-real-career-path/

https://www.ideatovalue.com/inno/nickskillicorn/2019/02/the-single-best-way-to-improve-your-brainstorming-sessions/

https://www.christiantoday.com/reporter/martin-saunder

https://thinkjarcollective.com/tools/thomas-edisons-creative-thinking-habits/

https://en.wikipedia.org/wiki/Arthur_D._Little

https://www.ideaconnection.com/thinking-m

About Kharis Publishing:

Kharis Publishing, an imprint of Kharis Media LLC, is a leading Christian and inspirational book publisher based in Aurora, Chicago metropolitan area, Illinois. Kharis' dual mission is to give voice to under-represented writers (including women and first-time authors) and equip orphans in developing countries with literacy tools. That is why, for each book sold, the publisher channels some of the proceeds into providing books and computers for orphanages in developing countries so that these kids may learn to read, dream, and grow. For a limited time, Kharis Publishing is accepting unsolicited queries for nonfiction (Christian, self-help, memoirs, business, health and wellness) from qualified leaders, professionals, pastors, and ministers. Learn more at: About Us - Kharis Publishing - Accepting Manuscript

Lightning Source UK Ltd.
Milton Keynes UK
UKHW020750010922
408173UK00009B/942